SPECTRUM®

Data Analysis and Probability

Grades 6–8

Published by Spectrum®
an imprint of Carson-Dellosa Publishing LLC
Greensboro, NC

Spectrum®
An imprint of Carson-Dellosa Publishing LLC
P.O. Box 35665
Greensboro, NC 27425 USA

ISBN 978-1-4838-1663-0

01-005157811

Table of Contents Data Analysis and Probability

Check What You Know

Probability Models

Determine the probabilities in each situation. Express each probability as a fraction in simplest form.

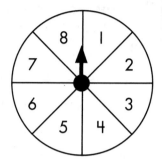

1. What is the probability of spinning a 3? _____

2. What is the probability of spinning an odd number? _____

3. What is the probability that a cube any color but red is picked from a bag containing 5 red cubes, 3 yellow cubes, and 2 white cubes? _____

4. A spinner has 12 equally spaced sections numbered 1 through 12. If it is spun, what is the probability of it landing on a number divisible by 3? _____

5. A purse contains the following coins: 12 pennies, 3 nickels, and 5 dimes.

    a. Which coin has the highest probability of being randomly selected? _____

    b. What is that probability? _____

Write *yes* or *no* to tell if each situation describes uniform probability.

6. selecting a student from a class of 10 boys and 15 girls _____

7. selecting a letter from the word "palace" _____

8. rolling a number with a 6-sided die _____

Solve the problems below. Express each probability as a fraction in simplest form.

9. A file cabinet contains 3 white folders, 2 red folders, 5 blue folders, and 3 green folders.

    What is the probability of randomly choosing a blue or red folder? _____

10. In a simulation of tossing a coin, a random number generator generates 255 zeros and 245 ones. Zero represents heads and one represents tails.

    a. What is the experimental probability of tossing a coin and getting heads? _____

    b. Which is greater, the experimental or theoretical probability of getting heads? _____

Lesson 1.1 Understanding Probability

An **experiment** is an activity in which results are observed. Each round of an experiment is called a **trial**, and the result of a trial is called an **outcome**. A set of one or more outcomes is called an **event**.

The **probability** of an event is a measure of the likelihood that the event will occur. This measure ranges from 0 to 1 and can be written as a ratio, fraction, decimal, or percent. To calculate probability, you must first know the number of possible outcomes.

The possible outcomes when you roll a die are the following: 1, 2, 3, 4, 5, and 6.

Every outcome is equally likely.

There is no chance that you can roll a 7.

Answer each question below based on the experiment described.

	a	b

1. You flip a coin.

    Possible outcomes?   Outcomes equally likely? (*Yes* or *no*)

    _____   _____

2. You roll a pair of dice and find the sum.

    Possible outcomes?   An impossible outcome?

    _____   _____

3. A bowl contains 15 red marbles and 5 green marbles.

    Possible outcomes?   Most likely outcome?

    _____   _____

4. Twenty names are written on slips of paper in a basket.

    Possible outcomes?   Outcomes equally likely? (*Yes* or *no*)

    _____   _____

Lesson 1.1 Understanding Probability

An **outcome** is a possible result of an activity or experiment. **Probability** is a measure of how likely it is that a specific outcome will occur. To find probability, create a ratio comparing the number of a specific outcome with the total number of possible outcomes.

$$\text{Probability } (P) = \frac{\text{number of a specific outcome}}{\text{number of possible outcomes}}$$

A bag contains 12 marbles: 7 blue and 5 red. If you choose a marble at random, the probability that it will be red is:

$$\text{Probability } (P) = \frac{5}{12} \quad \longleftarrow \text{ number of a specific outcome} \\ \longleftarrow \text{ number of possible outcomes}$$

You can express probability as a ratio, fraction, decimal, or percent.

When tossing a coin, what is the probability that it will land on heads?

specific outcome: heads

possible outcomes: heads, tails

probability of heads: $1:2$, $\frac{1}{2}$, 0.5, or 50%

Find the probability. Express your answer as a fraction in simplest form.

If you spin the spinner at right, what is the probability that the spinner will stop on each of the following?

1.   a number _____

2.   an even number _____

3.   an odd number _____

4.   a consonant _____

5.   a vowel _____

6.   the number 6 _____

7.   a number < 6 _____

8.   a number > 6 _____

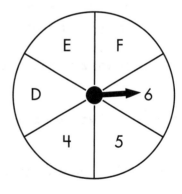

Lesson 1.1 Understanding Probability

Solve the problems based on one spin of the spinner. Express each probability as a fraction in simplest form.

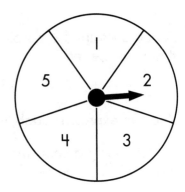

1. The number of possible outcomes is _____.

2. The probability of stopping on 4 is _____.

3. The probability of stopping on an odd number is _____.

4. The probability of not stopping on an odd number is _____.

5. The probability of stopping on 5 or 3 is _____.

6. The probability of stopping on a number > 1 is _____.

Solve each problem. Express probabilities as fractions in simplest form.

A bag contains 3 pennies, 2 nickels, and 4 dimes. You will select a coin at random.

7. The probability that you will choose a nickel is _____.

8. The probability that you will choose either a penny or a dime is _____.

9. The probability that you will not choose a penny is _____.

10. The probability that you will choose a coin worth more than 10 cents is _____.

Lesson 1.1 Understanding Probability

Solve each problem. Express each probability as a fraction in simplest form.

A box contains 3 red balls, 1 white ball, and 3 green balls. You pick one item at random.

11. The probability that you will choose 1 green ball is _____.

12. The probability that you will choose 1 white ball is _____.

The names of 8 girls and 7 boys are written on slips of paper, which are placed in a hat. The teacher will choose names at random to decide the order in which students will present their projects.

13. The probability that a girl will be chosen first is _____.

14. The probability that a boy will be chosen first is _____.

A snack shop sells hamburgers and turkey burgers with a choice of buns. The tree diagram shows all possible combinations. Use the diagram to answer the questions.

15. There are _____ possible combinations.

16. If you choose a sandwich at random, the probability that you will choose a turkey burger on a wheat bun is _____.

17. The probability that you will choose a sandwich on rye is _____.

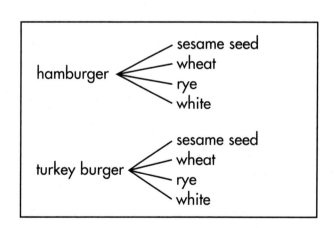

Lesson 1.2 Calculating Probability

An **event** is a set of possible outcomes from an activity or experiment. **Sample space** is the set of all possible outcomes of an activity or experiment. An event is a subset of sample space. Suppose you roll a 6-sided die once. The sample space is {1, 2, 3, 4, 5, 6}. You might roll a 2. Thus, one event of this experiment is {2}. If you roll the die twice, you might get a 3 and a 6. Thus, the set {3, 6} is one possible event of rolling the die twice.

Mutually exclusive events are events that cannot occur at the same time. If one event occurs, none of the other events will occur. If you roll a die and get a 6, you cannot get a 1, 2, 3, 4, or 5 at the same time.

If Events A and B are mutually exclusive, then the probability of A *or* B occurring is:

$$P(A) + P(B)$$

In one roll of a die, the probability of getting a 3 is $\frac{1}{6}$ and the probability of getting a 4 is also $\frac{1}{6}$. The probability of getting either a 3 or a 4 in one roll is $\frac{1}{6} + \frac{1}{6} = \frac{2}{6} = \frac{1}{3}$.

Complementary events are events that together make up the entire sample space. The probabilities of complementary events add up to 1, or 100%. Complementary events are mutually exclusive, but not all mutually exclusive events are complementary.

If A' is the complement of A, then the probability of A occurring is:

$$P(A) = 1 - P(A')$$

In one roll of a die, the probability of getting a 3 is $\frac{1}{6}$. Therefore, the probability of not getting a 3 is $1 - \frac{1}{6} = \frac{5}{6}$.

Determine each probability. Express your answer as a fraction in simplest form.

1. On one roll of a 6-sided die, what is the probability of getting a 1, 2, 4, or 6?

   The probability of getting a 1, 2, 4, or 6 is _____.

2. A bag holds 3 red marbles, 2 green marbles, and 3 black marbles. What is the probability of not choosing a black marble?

   The probability of not choosing a black marble is _____.

3. Events A and B are mutually exclusive. $P(A) = \frac{3}{10}$. P(B) is $\frac{1}{5}$. What is the probability that either A or B will occur?

   P(A) or P(B) is _____.

4. Events X, Y, and Z are complementary. $P(X) = \frac{1}{8}$. $P(Y) = \frac{1}{2}$. What is the probability that Z will occur?

   P(Z) is _____.

Lesson 1.2 Calculating Probability

Probability can also be thought of as the ratio of desired outcome(s) to the sample space. It can be expressed as a ratio, fraction, decimal, or percent.

When tossing a coin, what is the probability that it will land on heads?

desired outcome: heads   sample space: heads, tails   probability: 1:2, $\frac{1}{2}$, 50%, 0.5

Find the probability. Write answers as fractions in simplest form.

A box contains 3 red pencils, 4 blue pencils, 2 green pencils, and 1 regular pencil. If you take 1 pencil without looking, what is the probability of picking each of the following?

1. a red pencil _____

2. a blue pencil _____

3. a green pencil _____

4. a regular pencil _____

If you spin the spinner shown at the right, what is the probability of the spinner stopping on each of the following?

5. a letter _____

6. an odd number _____

7. an even number _____

8. a vowel _____

9. the number 3 _____

10. a consonant _____

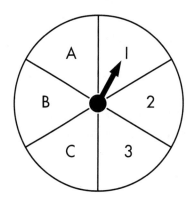

Lesson 1.2 Calculating Probability

Determine the probability for each of the following events. Write answers as fractions in simplest form.

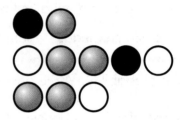

1. drawing a gray marble _____

2. drawing a white marble _____

3. drawing a black marble _____

4. drawing either a gray or a black marble _____

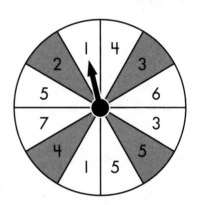

5. spinning a gray section _____

6. spinning a 4 _____

7. spinning a 1 _____

8. spinning *either* a 4 or 5 _____

9. spinning an even number _____

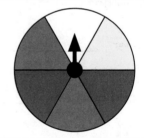

10. spinning a red section _____

11. spinning a blue section _____

12. spinning a yellow section _____

A jar contains 25 pennies, 20 nickels, and 15 dimes. If someone picks one coin without looking, what are the chances that they will pick the following:

13. penny _____

14. nickel _____

15. dime _____

Lesson 1.3 Uniform Probability Models

When all outcomes of an experiment are equally likely, the event has **uniform probability**.

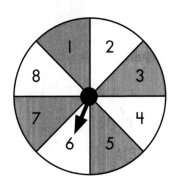

This spinner has 8 equally divided sections. Every time it is used, there is an equal chance ($\frac{1}{8}$) that it will land on any given number.

Chance of spinning 6 — $\frac{1}{8}$

Chance of spinning 3 — $\frac{1}{8}$

Chance of spinning 7 — $\frac{1}{8}$

Write *yes* or *no* to tell if each situation describes a uniform probability model.

	a	b
1.	rolling one die	rolling two dice
2.	flipping a coin	a spinner with 3 stars and 2 diamonds
3.	calling on a girl in class	calling on any student in class
4.	winning the lottery	drawing an 8 from a deck of cards
5.	calling on a boy in class	a spinner with 5 red and 2 blue sections
6.	flipping a coin and rolling a die	a spinner with 3 squares and 3 triangles

Lesson 1.3 Uniform Probability Models

When all outcomes of an experiment are equally likely, the event has **uniform probability**.

To create a uniform probability problem, divide the event into equal sections of different possibilities.

Color one section red. Color one section yellow. Color one section blue. Color one section green.

There is a $\frac{1}{4}$ chance of spinning red, blue, yellow, or green.

This is an example of a spinner that has uniform probability.

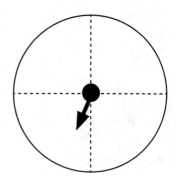

Follow the directions to set up uniform probabilities.

1. Draw a spinner that has an equal chance of spinning a star or a diamond.

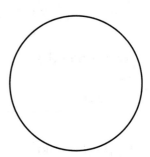

2. Draw a spinner that has an equal chance of spinning a number 1 through 4.

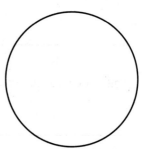

3. Color the marbles so that there is an equal chance of pulling a blue or green marble.

4. Draw shapes in the bag so that there is an equal chance of pulling a triangle, a square, and a circle.

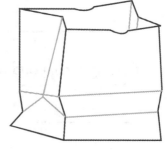

NAME _____

Lesson 1.4 Other Probability Models

When an event does not have uniform probability, the odds of each particular outcome are not equally likely.

When using this spinner, there is a greater chance of landing in the blue section than there is of landing in the red or white sections.

Chance of spinning blue — $\frac{1}{2}$

Chance of spinning red — $\frac{1}{4}$

Chance of spinning white — $\frac{1}{4}$

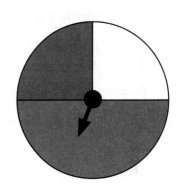

For each situation pictured, state if the odds of all outcomes are *equal* or *not equal*.

<table>
<tr><td align="center">**a**</td><td align="center">**b**</td></tr>
</table>

1. 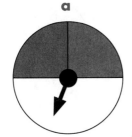 _____   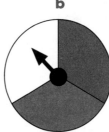 _____

2. _____   _____

3. _____   _____

4. _____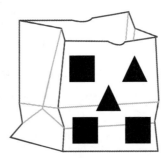

Lesson 1.4   Other Probability Models

When a probability has unequal odds, it can be written as a fraction or a ratio.

A game is being played in which the spinner must land on a star to win.

Spinner 1 — $\frac{2}{6}$ or $\frac{1}{3}$ chance of spinning a star

Spinner 2 — $\frac{3}{6}$ or $\frac{1}{2}$ chance of spinning a star

$\frac{1}{3} < \frac{1}{2}$, so the greatest chance of winning is using spinner 2.

Spinner 1   Spinner 2

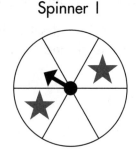

Circle the game with the best odds of winning. Show your work.

1. Spin an even number:

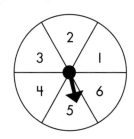
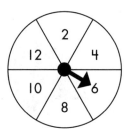

2. Spin the color blue.

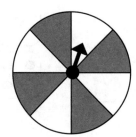
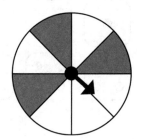

3. Choose a gray marble.

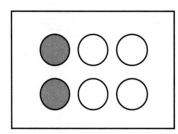
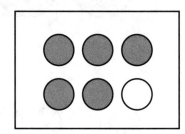

Lesson 1.4 Other Probability Models

Solve the problems below.

1. A spinner has 6 sections of equal size. One is red, two are blue, and 3 are yellow.

   a. If you spin one time, what are the odds that you will land on blue? _____

   b. What are the odds that you will land on yellow? _____

2. You flip a coin that has a heads side and a tails side.

   a. What are the odds that the coin will land on heads the first time you flip it? _____

   b. You have flipped the coin 50 times. You have landed on heads 31 times and tails

      19 times. What are the odds that the coin will land on tails on the next flip? _____

3. At the school festival, you can win a bicycle by pulling a red ball out of a bag. The first bag has 52 white balls, 27 green balls, and 11 red balls. The second bag has 25 white balls, 25 green balls, 25 yellow balls, and 10 red balls.

   a. What are the odds of pulling a red ball from the first bag? _____

   b. What are the odds of pulling a red ball from the second bag? _____

   c. Which bag has the best odds? _____

4. A bag contains 9 green marbles and 16 red marbles. You will choose one marble out of the bag without looking.

   a. What are the odds of choosing a red marble? _____

   b. You do not replace marbles after they are chosen. So far you have chosen 4 red marbles and 2 green marbles. What are the odds of choosing a red marble now? _____

Lesson 1.5 Comparing Experimental and Theoretical Probabilities

Probability is a number between 0 and 1—written as a fraction, a decimal, or a percent—that gives the likelihood of an event occurring. An event is a situation that can occur in different ways. The possible ways that an event can occur are called **outcomes**. **Theoretical probability** can be defined as $\frac{\text{\# of desired outcomes}}{\text{total \# of outcomes}}$.

Experimental probability is probability that is based on a certain number of events or **trials** that have been conducted in an experiment. **Relative frequency** is the observed number of successful trials divided by the total number of trials. Experimental probability can be defined as $\frac{\text{\# of successful trials}}{\text{total \# of trials}}$. As the number of trials increases, the experimental probability gets closer to the theoretical probability. This phenomenon is called the **Law of Large Numbers**.

For example, the theoretical probability of flipping heads on a coin is $\frac{1}{2}$ or 50%. Suppose you flipped a coin 20 times and 5 out of those times the coin landed on "heads." The experimental probability is $\frac{5}{20} = \frac{1}{4}$. This is smaller than the theoretical probability of $\frac{1}{2}$. The Law of Large Numbers states that as you increase the number of trials, the experimental probability gets closer to the theoretical probability. So for this example, if the number of trials is increased, the experimental probability would get closer to $\frac{1}{2}$.

Find the following experimental probabilities. Express each probability as a fraction in simplest form.

1. Out of 90 raffle tickets for a free visit to a salon, 15 are winners. What is the experimental

   probability of winning a free visit? _____

2. The experimental probability of an event occurring is 75%. If the number of trials is 120,

   what is the number of trials for which the event does *not* occur? _____

3. There are 30 people in a movie theater, 18 of whom are male. What is the probability that

   the next person who comes into the theater will be a woman? _____

Find the following theoretical probabilities. Express each probability as a fraction in simplest form.

4. For a 12-month calendar, what is the probability of turning to the month of February or

   September? _____

5. If a card is drawn from a stack of cards numbered 1 through 10, what is the probability of

   selecting a card greater than 6? _____

6. What is the probability of flipping a coin to heads twice? _____

Lesson 1.5 Comparing Experimental and Theoretical Probabilities

Compare the theoretical probability to the experimental probability. Express each probability as a fraction in simplest form.

7. Allison rolls a die numbered 1 through 6. The results are shown in the table below.

   a. What is the experimental probability of rolling a 6?

   _____

   b. What is the theoretical probability of rolling a 6? _____

   c. Which probability is greater? _____

   How much greater? _____

   d. What is the experimental probability of rolling an even number? _____

   e. What is the theoretical probability of rolling an even number? _____

   f. Which probability is greater? _____ How much greater? _____

Result	Frequency
1	4
2	9
3	7
4	8
5	5
6	3

8. Allison continues to roll the die. The results are shown in the table below.

   a. What is the experimental probability of rolling a 6?

   _____

   b. What is the theoretical probability of rolling a 6? _____

   c. Which probability is greater? _____

   How much greater? _____

   d. What is the experimental probability of rolling an even number? _____

   e. What is the theoretical probability of rolling an even number? _____

   f. Which probability is greater? _____ How much greater? _____

Result	Frequency
1	23
2	22
3	22
4	25
5	28
6	24

Lesson 1.6 Simulations

Some real-life situations may be time-consuming, too expensive, impractical, or difficult to analyze using a statistical study. In these situations, simulations are often used to model the real-life events. A **simulation** is a method of modeling random events by using random numbers, so that simulated events correspond to real-world events. The random numbers used in a simulation can be obtained using random number generators, dice, coins, marbles in a jar, pieces of papers, or spinners. The most commonly used tool to create a simulation is a random number generator. Random numbers generators can be found on the Internet, on graphing calculators, in spreadsheets, and in computer mathematics software.

Solve the problems below. Express all probabilities in decimal form, rounded to the nearest hundredth.

1. Carlos used a random number generator on the Internet to simulate flipping a coin 50 times. He generated 50 random zeros and ones, with 0 being the outcome heads and 1 being the outcome tails. The numbers Carlos generated are shown in the chart.

0	0	1	0	1	1	0	1	1	0
1	1	0	0	1	0	0	1	1	1
0	0	0	1	0	1	1	1	1	0
1	0	1	1	1	0	0	0	1	1
0	0	1	1	1	1	1	1	0	1

Based on the results of the simulation, what is the probability of getting heads? _____

2. Carlos decided to perform the simulation 50 more times for a total of 100 trials. The next set of 50 numbers are shown in the chart.

0	0	0	1	0	1	0	1	1	1
0	1	1	0	1	1	0	0	0	1
1	1	1	0	0	0	1	1	1	1
1	1	0	0	1	1	0	0	1	0
1	0	0	1	1	1	0	0	0	0

Based on the results of the 100 trials, what is

the probability of getting heads? _____

Is the probability of getting heads closer to the theoretical probability after 100 trials than it

was after 50 trials? _____

3. In basketball, Keisha has made 80% of her free throws. She is performing a simulation to find the experimental probability of making a basket on her next 25 free throws. Because her free throw

8	4	4	4	8	9	7	6	3
3	3	5	3	5	1	7	4	0
8	4	7	4	2	7	8	6	1

percentage is 80%, that means she makes 8 out of 10 free throws. For her simulation, she is going to generate random integers from 0 to 9 to represent the result of a free throw. The digits 0 to 7 will represent a successful free throw and the digits 8 and 9 will represent a missed free throw. The numbers generated for her simulation are shown above.

Based on the results of the simulation, what is the probability of Keisha making a free throw

on her next 25 shots? _____

Lesson 1.6 Simulations

When creating a simulation, the event has to be clearly defined, as does the success or failure of the event.

A store gives a coupon to every 15th customer for $1 off their next order. To simulate this real-life situation, you can represent the next 15 customers by writing the numbers 1 through 15 on 15 different pieces of paper. Assign one of the numbers, for example, the number 1, to the customer who gets the coupon (success). The other 14 numbers represent customers who do not get the coupon (failure). You can find the experimental probability that a customer entering the store gets a coupon by repeating the process of selecting a random piece of paper, recording the result, and replacing the piece of paper that was selected.

Design a simulation to model each situation.

4. A baseball player has a 0.250 batting average. That means he averages 1 hit for every 4 at bats.

How can you simulate the player's turn at bat?

_____

What is a successful event in your simulation?

_____

What is a failure in your simulation?

_____

5. Create a simulation to find the probability of rolling an even number on a die numbered 1 through 6.

How can you simulate a roll of the die?

_____

What is a successful event in your simulation?

_____

What is a failure in your simulation?

_____

Check What You Learned

Probability Models

Determine the probabilities in each situation. Express each probability as a fraction in simplest form.

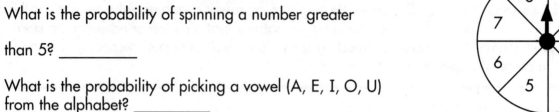

1. What is the probability of spinning a number less than 5? _____

2. What is the probability of spinning a number greater

   than 5? _____

3. What is the probability of picking a vowel (A, E, I, O, U) from the alphabet? _____

4. A letter is randomly selected from the name "Annie."

   a. What is the probability of selecting "N"? _____

   b. What is the probability of selecting "A"? _____

5. What is the probability of randomly selecting a prime number from the numbers 1 to 10,

   inclusive? _____

Write *yes* or *no* to tell if each situation describes uniform probability.

6. selecting head or tails when tossing a coin _____

7. selecting white or wheat bread in the supermarket _____

8. selecting "Monday," "Tuesday," "Wednesday," "Thursday," or "Friday" in the month of

   January _____

Solve the problem below. Express the probability as a fraction in simplest form.

9. A student kicks 50 penalty kicks in soccer practice and makes 39 goals. In the next practice, he kicks 50 penalty kicks and makes 40 goals. Based on both of his practices, what is the

   experimental probability that he will kick a goal on his next penalty kick? _____

Check What You Know

Calculating Probability and Compound Events

Create a tree diagram and then answer the questions.

1. Pepi's Pizza has a choice of thin crust or thick crust. The available toppings are mushrooms, onions, pepperoni, and sausage. Make a tree diagram showing the possible outcomes for a 1-topping pizza.

2. How many possible outcomes are there? _____

Solve the problems below. Express each probability as a fraction in simplest form.

3. Three numbers are chosen from the numbers 1 through 10, inclusive with replacement. What is the probability of selecting 3 odd numbers? _____

4. Justin has 3 white socks, 5 black socks, and 2 blue socks in his drawer. If he randomly selects two socks without replacement, what is the probability both socks are *not* black? _____

5. What is the probability of randomly selecting a 3-digit password that consists of three unique digits from 0 through 9, inclusive? _____

6. If two coins are tossed, what is the probability of both landing on tails? _____

7. A school cafeteria serves a choice of fish, chicken, or turkey and a choice of mashed potatoes or greens. What is the probability of randomly choosing a meal with chicken and mashed potatoes? _____

8. Liam has a deck of cards and a coin. The cards are numbered 1–13 and there are four for each number in the deck. What is the probability that he will pull a 9 from the deck of cards and that the coin will land on tails? _____

9. If a dress shop offers cotton, silk, satin, and polyester fabrics, what is the probability that its next 2 customers will choose a silk fabric? _____

10. A school offers an afternoon snack of grape juice, apple juice, or milk plus a chocolate chip cookie or an oatmeal and raisin cookie. What is the likelihood that a child will choose a juice and a chocolate chip cookie as a snack? _____

Lesson 2.1 Tree Diagrams

To calculate a probability, you need to know how many outcomes are possible. Recall that the set of all possible outcomes of an activity or experiment is the sample space. To help determine the sample space, organize the possibilities using a list, chart, or tree diagram.

Show the sample space for tossing a nickel, a dime, and a quarter.

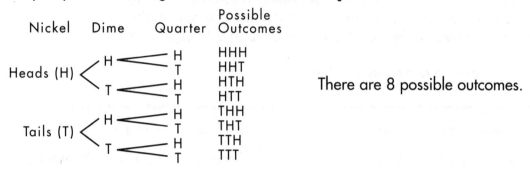

There are 8 possible outcomes.

If you tossed these 3 coins once, what is the probability of getting exactly 2 tails? Notice that 3 of the 8 possible outcomes have exactly 2 tails. The probability of getting exactly 2 tails is $\frac{3}{8}$.

Create a tree diagram and answer the question.

1. The chart below shows all possible outcomes of tossing 1 coin and rolling 1 die. In the space provided, create a tree diagram showing all possible outcomes. Begin with the outcomes of the coin toss. Then, connect these outcomes with each possible outcome of the roll of the die.

CHART

Coin

Die	Heads	Tails
1	H1	T1
2	H2	T2
3	H3	T3
4	H4	T4
5	H5	T5
6	H6	T6

TREE DIAGRAM

Coin   Die

The number of possible outcomes is _____.

Lesson 2.1 Tree Diagrams

Solve each problem. Express probabilities as fractions in simplest form.

1. A store sells T-shirts in the colors and sizes shown in the chart. Make a tree diagram.

Colors	Sizes
red	small
blue	medium
tie-dyed	large

Tree Diagram

a. There are _____ possible outcomes, or choices, of T-shirts.

b. Suppose the store has just 1 of each size and color. If you select a T-shirt at random, the probability that you will choose a large shirt is _____.

2. The tree diagram below shows the combinations of colors, styles, and speeds of bicycles available at a bicycle shop. You select one at random.

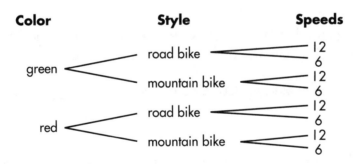

a. There are _____ combinations of bicycles from which to choose.

b. The probability of choosing a green bicycle is _____.

c. The probability of choosing a 6-speed mountain bicycle is _____.

d. The probability of choosing a red, 12-speed road bicycle is _____.

Lesson 2.2 Calculating Probability

A **compound event** consists of two or more events. Tossing two coins is a compound event. Tossing a coin and rolling a die is also a compound event.

Compound events are **independent** if the outcome of one event does not influence the outcome of the others. When you flip a coin, there is a $\frac{1}{2}$ probability of heads and a $\frac{1}{2}$ probability of tails. Suppose your coin flip produces tails. If you flip the coin again, there is still a $\frac{1}{2}$ probability of heads and a $\frac{1}{2}$ probability of tails. These events are independent.

If events A and B are independent, then the probability of both occurring is:

$P(A) \times P(B)$

The probability of getting tails in one coin flip is $\frac{1}{2}$. The probability of getting a 5 in one roll of a die is $\frac{1}{6}$. The probability of both occurring, {tails, 5}, is $\frac{1}{2} \times \frac{1}{6} = \frac{1}{12}$.

Determine each probability. Express your answer as a fraction in simplest form.

1. Events E and F are independent. The probability that E will occur is $\frac{2}{5}$. The probability that F will occur is $\frac{3}{7}$. What is the probability that both E and F will occur?

   The probability that both E and F will occur is _____.

2. A nationwide poll found that 3 of 5 voters planned to vote for Candidate X. Jay and Aisha voted. What is the probability that both voted for Candidate X?

   The probability that both voted for Candidate X is _____.

3. You roll a 6-sided die and flip a coin. What is the probability of getting an even number on the die and heads on the coin?

   P(even) and P(heads) is _____.

4. A jar of jellybeans has 6 blue, 2 orange, and 8 red jellybeans. You choose 1 jellybean, put it back, and then choose another. What is the probability that you choose 2 blue jellybeans?

   The probability of choosing 2 blue jellybeans is _____.

Lesson 2.2 Calculating Probability

Two events are **dependent** if the outcome of one event influences the outcome of the other. If events A and B are dependent, then the probability of both occurring is:

$$P(A) \times P(B \text{ after } A \text{ occurs})$$

Suppose a bag holds 2 yellow golf balls and 2 white golf balls. Each color of ball has a $\frac{2}{4}$ or $\frac{1}{2}$ chance of being selected. You take a yellow ball out of the bag and do not replace it. Now, there are 2 white balls and 1 yellow ball. The probability of choosing a white ball next is $\frac{2}{3}$. Therefore, the probability of choosing a yellow ball, P(A), and then a white ball, P(B after A occurs), is $\frac{1}{2} \times \frac{2}{3} = \frac{2}{6} = \frac{1}{3}$.

Determine each probability. Express your answer as a fraction in simplest form.

1. A jar of jellybeans has 6 blue, 2 orange, and 8 red jellybeans. You choose 1 jellybean and eat it. You then choose another and eat it. What is the probability that you ate 2 blue jellybeans?

    The probability that you ate 2 blue jellybeans is _____.

2. A bowl contains 20 raffle tickets, including 1 winning ticket. You take 1 ticket from the bowl. Your friend then takes 1 ticket from the bowl. What are the chances that both you and your friend picked losing tickets?

    The probability of both of you picking losing tickets is _____.

3. A box holds 5 electronic games. Two of the games are defective. You take 1 game from the box. Without replacing it, you choose another game from the box. How likely is it that you picked 2 defective games?

    There is a _____ probability that both games are defective.

4. A set of 12 cards contains an equal number of clubs, diamonds, hearts, and spades. You take 3 cards in a row from the set without replacing them. What are the chances that all three are spades?

    The probability of 3 spades is _____.

Lesson 2.3 Understanding Compound Events

The **Fundamental Counting Principle** states that when an experiment has an event with more than one part, the number of possible outcomes is calculated by looking at the number of possible outcomes for each part. An event with more than one part is considered **a compound event**. The number of possible outcomes for the first element (*a*) can be multiplied by the number of possible outcomes for the second element (*b*) to find the total number of possible outcomes (*o*). So, $a \times b = o$.

There are 3 balls (yellow, red, and green) in one bag and 4 balls (purple, blue, white, and black) in another bag. If a person draws one ball from each bag, how many possible outcomes are there?

Step 1: Find the number of outcomes for the first event. 3

Step 2: Find the number of outcomes for the second event. 4

Step 3: Multiply these together. 3×4

Step 4: State the number of possible outcomes for the combined event. 12

Use the Fundamental Counting Principle to find the number of possible outcomes for each compound event described.

	a	b

1. rolling two dice that are numbered 1–6   flipping a coin and rolling a die numbered 1–6

_____   _____

2. spinning a 4-part spinner and flipping a coin   pulling a card from a full deck and flipping a coin

_____   _____

3. spinning a 6-part spinner and rolling a die numbered 1–6   flipping a coin and rolling two dice numbered 1–6

_____   _____

4. spinning a 4-part spinner and pulling a card from a full deck   flipping 2 coins and rolling 2 dice numbered 1–6

_____   _____

Lesson 2.3 Understanding Compound Events SHOW YOUR WORK

Use the Fundamental Counting Principle to find the number of possible outcomes. Show your work.

1. 3 coins are tossed and two six-sided dice are rolled. How many possible outcomes are there?

    There are _____ possible outcomes.

2. Jed is shopping. He is looking at 5 different ties, 3 different sweaters, and 4 different shirts. How many possible combinations can he make?

    Jed can make _____ possible combinations.

3. Miranda's jewelry box contains 8 necklaces, 10 pairs of earrings, and 4 bracelets. How many combinations, which contain all 3 kinds of jewelry, can she make?

    Miranda can make _____ combinations of jewelry.

4. Robert has to color in 4 different shapes (circle, square, triangle, and rectangle) and has 5 colors to choose from (green, yellow, red, blue, and orange). If he can only use each color one time, how many ways can he color the shapes?

    Robert can color the shapes _____ different ways.

5. Spencer needs to put on gloves, a hat, and a scarf. He has 5 hats, 4 pairs of gloves, and 9 scarves to choose from. How many combinations of gloves, hats, and scarves can Spencer make?

    Spencer can make _____ combinations.

6. Pilar wants to cook a meal that consists of a meat, a starch, and a vegetable. At the grocery store there are 8 choices of meat, 8 choices of vegetables, and 3 choices of starches. How many possible combinations can Pilar make?

    Pilar can make _____ combinations.

7. Jacob must collect a flower, a vegetable, and an herb. In the garden, there are 10 kinds of flowers, 7 kinds of vegetables, and 4 kinds of herbs. How many combinations can Jacob make?

    Jacob can make _____ combinations.

1.

2.

3.

4.

5.

6.

7.

Lesson 2.4 Representing Compound Events

A **sample space** is a set of all possible outcomes (or possible results) for an activity or experiment. To determine the sample space, it is helpful to organize the possibilities using a tree diagram, chart, or table.

Show the sample space for tossing a nickel, a dime, and a quarter, using a tree diagram.

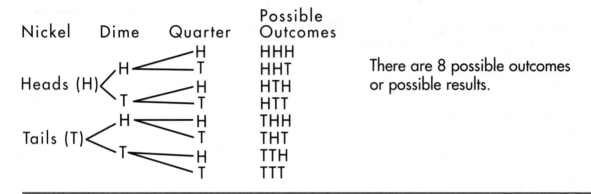

There are 8 possible outcomes or possible results.

Make a tree diagram for each situation. Determine the number of possible outcomes.

1. The concession stand offers the drink choices shown in the table.

Drinks	Sizes
Lemonade	Small
Fruit Punch	Medium
Apple Cider	Large
	Jumbo

   There are _____ possible outcomes.

2. The Kellys are planning their vacation activities. On the first day, they can go to the zoo or the museum. On the second day, they can go to the pier or the dunes. On the third day, they have to choose sailing, swimming, or horseback riding.

   There are _____ possible outcomes.

Lesson 2.4 Representing Compound Events

One way to show sample space for compound events is with a chart. What is the sample space if you roll 1 die and flip 1 coin?

Penny

	Heads	Tails
1	H1	T1
2	H2	T2
3	H3	T3
4	H4	T4
5	H5	T5
6	H6	T6

Die

What is the sample space? It is 12, because there are 12 possible outcomes.

Solve each problem.

1. Juan flips a penny, a nickel, and a dime at the same time. How many different combinations of heads and tails can he get?

_____

2. Latisha has red, blue, and black sneakers; blue, tan, and white pants; and black and gray sweatshirts. How many different outfits can she make?

_____

3. Jonathan, Kaitlin, and Ling are trying to decide in what order they should appear during their talent show performance. They made this chart showing the possible orders. Can you show the same results using a tree diagram? (Remember, each person can appear only once in the 1, 2, 3 order.) What is the total number of possible orders?

_____

1	2	3
J	K	L
K	L	J
L	K	J
J	L	K
K	J	L
L	J	K

Lesson 2.4 Representing Compound Events

Tables can be used to represent compound events that have two elements.

John rolls two dice. What is the probability that he will roll a sum of nine?

Step 1: Create a table with rows that match one part of the event and columns that match the other part of the event.

Step 2: Fill in the headers for your table with the possible outcomes for each part of the event.

Step 3: Fill in the table with the possible final outcomes.

Step 4: Find the total number of possible final outcomes (36) and the number of final outcomes with the desired characteristic (4) to calculate the probability.

Possible Outcomes Die #1

	1	2	3	4	5	6
1	2	3	4	5	6	7
2	3	4	5	6	7	8
3	4	5	6	7	8	9
4	5	6	7	8	9	10
5	6	7	8	9	10	11
6	7	8	9	10	11	12

(Possible Outcomes Die #2)

The shaded numbers are the final outcomes, or sums, when the outcomes are added together.

The probability is $\frac{4}{36}$, or $\frac{1}{9}$.

Create a table to solve the problems.

1. Erin is getting dressed in the morning. She is choosing from 4 skirts (black, brown, blue, and khaki) and 5 sweaters (black, blue, red, green, and yellow). What is the probability that she will wear both black and blue?

2. Michael is playing a game in which he must spin a spinner numbered 1–8 first, and then roll a die numbered 1–6. What is the probability that he will spin and roll a sum of 10?

Lesson 2.5 Problem Solving

Solve each problem using the Fundamental Counting Principle.

1. Stephen flips a coin and pulls a marble from a bag which contains equal amounts of red, green, yellow, and blue marbles. How many outcomes are possible?

   There are _____ possible outcomes.

   1.

2. Julie is playing a game. She has a bag with cards numbered 1–10 and another bag with red and yellow bouncy balls. She pulls a number card out of one bag and a bouncy ball out of another bag. How many outcomes are possible?

   There are _____ possible outcomes.

   2.

3. At the sandwich shop, Nick can order a sandwich on a sub roll, wheat bread, or a Kaiser roll. He can have ham, turkey, or roast beef. Then, he can add cheese, lettuce, or pickles. What is the probability that he will have a sandwich that is both on wheat bread and made with ham?

   There is a _____ chance of his ordering a sandwich with both wheat bread and ham.

   3.

4. Jeff has a deck of cards and a coin. What is the chance that he will pull a 10 from the deck of cards and land on heads?

   There is a _____ chance of Jeff pulling a 10 and flipping heads at the same time?

   4.

Lesson 2.5 Problem Solving

Solve each problem using a tree diagram.

1. Mark and his friends are playing a game. They take turns pulling a number 1–5 out of one bag and a number 6–10 out of another bag. They keep their score and then put the numbers back. The first person to get a sum of 15 wins. What is the probability of winning on each turn?

   There is a _____ chance of winning the game on each turn.

   1.

2. Mr. Roberts' son has a set of blocks that are made up of 12 different shapes and 4 different colors. Every shape comes in every color. How many blocks are in the set?

   There are _____ blocks in the set.

   2.

3. Sarah is at the smoothie shop. She can choose a base of ice, banana, or yogurt. She can add blueberries, strawberries, or mangoes. Then, she can add honey, protein powder, or kale. How many combinations are possible?

   Sarah has _____ combinations to choose from.

   3.

4. A box of chocolates is half milk chocolate and half dark chocolate. Each kind of chocolate is filled with coconut, caramel, nuts, or cherries. What is the probability of choosing a candy that is made of dark chocolate and cherries?

   There is a _____ chance of choosing a candy made of dark chocolate and cherries.

   4.

Lesson 2.5 Problem Solving

Solve each problem using a table.

1. A cube with six sides has the letters A–F on it. A spinner has the letters G–L on it. How many letter combinations are there when the cube is rolled and the spinner is spun?

   There are _____ possible letter combinations.

2. A bakery has both donuts and bagels. They are each available in blueberry, chocolate, and plain. What is the probability of choosing at random a blueberry bagel?

   There is a _____ chance of randomly choosing a blueberry bagel.

3. Customers have a choice of thin crust, hand-tossed crust, or deep dish pizzas. They can add a pesto, tomato, or olive oil base. Finally, they can add pepperoni, mushrooms, or onions. What is the probability that a customer will order a pizza with both thin crust and mushrooms?

   There is a _____ chance that a customer will order a pizza with both thin crust and mushrooms.

4. Katie is trying to decide where to go on vacation. She has narrowed it down to Spain, Hawaii, and Puerto Rico. She can take between 7 and 10 days for her trip. How many options does she have?

   Katie has _____ choices for her vacation.

1.

2.

3.

4.

Lesson 2.5   Problem Solving

Solve each problem. Write your answer as a fraction in simplest form.

1. You roll a 6-sided die. What is the probability that you will roll a 4?

    The probability is _____.

2. What is the probability of getting either a 2 or a 5?

    The probability is _____.

3. What is the probability that you will not roll a 6?

    The probability is _____.

4. You roll a pair of 6-sided dice once. What is the probability that you will roll two 3s?

    The probability is _____.

Each of 10 bins contains 1 piece of fruit. Two bins are oranges, 3 are apples, 4 are peaches, and 1 is a melon. You pick a bin without looking at its contents.

5. What is the probability that you chose an orange?

    The probability is _____.

6. What is the probability that you chose either an apple or a peach?

    The probability is _____.

7. You take 1 fruit from a bin and do not replace it. Then, you pick another fruit. What is the probability that you chose two peaches?

    The probability is _____.

8. What is the probability that you did not choose two peaches?

    The probability is _____.

Lesson 2.5 Problem Solving

Solve each problem. Express probabilities as a percent, rounded to the nearest tenth.

1. Jamie will spin the spinner 1 time. He will also flip a coin 1 time. Complete the chart of all possible outcomes from this experiment. Two outcomes are given in the chart as examples. Then, draw a tree diagram showing all possible outcomes.

CHART

TREE DIAGRAM

Coin   Spinner

Coin

Spinner	Heads	Tails
	H1	T1

2. This experiment has _____ possible outcomes.

3. What is the probability of getting heads on the coin flip and a 2 on the spin?

    The probability is _____%.

4. What is the probability of not getting heads and a 2?

    The probability is _____%.

5. What is the probability of getting tails and an odd number?

    The probability is _____%.

NAME _____

 Check What You Learned

Calculating Probability and Compound Events

CHAPTER 2 POSTTEST

Solve each problem. Express probabilities as fractions in simplest form.

A deck of playing cards has 52 cards and 4 suits: clubs, diamonds, hearts, and spades. Each suit has an equal number of cards. The cards range from 2 through ace in each suit. You draw 1 card at random. What is the probability that the card is:

1. a jack? _____

2. a club? _____

3. either an ace or a diamond? _____

4. not a spade? _____

You draw 1 card at random, replace it, and then draw another card. What is the probability that you drew:

5. a king and a 9? _____

6. a spade and a heart? _____

7. a 2 and a diamond? _____

You draw 1 card at random and do not replace it. You then draw another card. What is the probability that you drew:

8. a queen and then a 5? _____

9. a club and then a spade? _____

Check What You Learned

Calculating Probability and Compound Events

Solve each problem. Express probabilities as fractions in simplest form.

You are serving cheese at a party. The tray holds 6 cheddar cubes, 5 Swiss cubes, and 8 provolone cubes. If each person chooses 1 cube at random, what is the probability that:

10. both the first and second person chose cheddar? _____

11. the first person chose Swiss and the second chose provolone? _____

12. At a restaurant, you can choose a chicken, steak, or fish dinner. With each dinner you have a choice of a salad or fruit. Each dinner also comes with rice or a potato. If you choose a dinner at random, create a tree diagram showing all possible outcomes.

Use your tree diagram to answer the following questions. Express probabilities as percents, rounded to the nearest tenth.

13. How many possible outcomes are there? _____

What is the probability of choosing a dinner with:

14. fruit? _____%

15. steak and potato? _____%

16. fish, salad, and rice? _____%

NAME _____

Check What You Know

Statistical Thinking

Read each question and write *statistical* or *not statistical*.

1. How often do students in my class text? _____

2. What is my favorite subject? _____

3. What is the most popular hair style observed on the street? _____

4. How tall is the statue in front of the building? _____

Tell if each sample would be considered *random* or *biased*.

5. Every tenth customer at an art festival is asked about his or her favorite artist.

    _____

6. One thousand citizens from different neighborhoods are asked in a survey if they would

    approve of a citywide recycling program. _____

7. Every third person walking by on the street in front of a library is asked if they would rather

    have e-books instead of library books. _____

Solve the problems.

8. A spinner with three equal sections has a circle, rectangle, and diamond on each section, respectively. If the spinner lands on a diamond 15 out of 50 times, how many times would it be expected to land on a diamond the next 100 spins?

    _____

9. Out of 2,000 people interviewed at a mall, 700 of them had made a purchase. How many of the next 500 people would you expect to have made purchases?

    _____

10. In basketball practice, a student missed 30 out of 50 baskets. What is the probability of the baskets the student will make at the next practice?

    _____

Lesson 3.1 Asking Statistical Questions

A **statistical question** has answers that will vary.

"How old are the students in my school?" is a statistical question because not every answer will be the same.

"How old am I?" is not a statistical question because there is only one answer.

Read each question and write *statistical* or *not statistical*.

	a	b
1.	How tall are the students in my class?	What does this apple cost?
	_____	_____
2.	What grades did students score on the test?	How fast can dogs run 100 yards?
	_____	_____
3.	How many marbles are in the jar?	Does a chocolate bar weigh more than a pack of jelly beans?
	_____	_____
4.	What was the difference in rainfall between March and April?	How many miles can cars travel on a gallon of gas?
	_____	_____
5.	Will I score a basket in the game tonight?	How often do adults eat breakfast?
	_____	_____

Lesson 3.1 Asking Statistical Questions

Write one statistical question for each category below.

I. height of students

_____

2. test scores

_____

3. number of pages in books

_____

4. number of students in classes

_____

5. price of apples

_____

6. type of automobile

_____

7. exercise

_____

Lesson 3.2 Designing a Study

Step 1: Ask a question
What do you want to learn from your study? Be specific. For example, you might want to know which brand of tomato soup is most nutritious. Your question might be: Which brand of tomato soup provides the most protein with the least fat?

Step 2: Identify your sample
Identify the population you want to study. A **population** is the set of all items of interest to your study. A population might be all students in your school or all brands of tomato soup offered for sale in your town.

You probably cannot collect data from every member of the population. Instead, you can collect data from a **sample**, or part of the population. The sample must accurately represent the whole population. You want to be able to draw conclusions about the population based on the sample. A sample is **biased** if it does not accurately represent the population. In the soup example, our sample might be all brands of tomato soup offered for sale at three stores in your community.

Step 3: Collect data
First, identify the data you want to collect. **Data** are items of information, such as facts or statistics. In our study, we want data on protein and fat.

Next, decide how to collect the data. If you want to gather information from people, you could write questions for members of your sample to answer. To gather data about soup, you might go to three stores. You would record all brands of tomato soup on the shelves and the amounts of protein and fat in each brand.

Step 4: Analyze data
Organize your data in a meaningful way, such as in a table. This table organizes grams of protein and fat in tomato soup.

Nutrition Facts about Tomato Soup in grams (g)		
Brand	**Protein**	**Total Fat**
X	5 g	2 g
Y	6 g	4 g
Z	2 g	1 g

How can you analyze this data to determine the answer to your question: Which brand provides the most protein with the least fat? One way is to use fractions to find the total fat per gram of protein in each brand. Then, convert the factions to decimals to make them easier to compare.

Brand X: 2 g fat/5 g protein = 0.4 g fat per gram of protein

Brand Y: 4 g fat/6 g protein = 0.7 g fat per gram of protein (rounded)

Brand Z: 1 g fat/2 g protein = 0.5 g fat per gram of protein

Step 5: Interpret results
From your analysis, you could conclude that Brand X is the most nutritious soup, because it contains the least fat per gram of protein.

Lesson 3.2 Designing a Study

Now, design your own study.

Step 1: Ask a question. What is the most popular _____ among males and females? You fill in the blank. For example, you might fill in *pet, color,* or *sport.*

Step 2: Identify your sample. Choose a sample of 20 people, 10 males and 10 females. You can include family, friends, and classmates.

Step 3: Collect data. List 4 choices within the category you chose. For example, if your category is *pet,* you might list *cat, dog, snake,* and *bird.* Design a survey form that lists the choices and asks people to rank them from 1 (least favorite) to 4 (most favorite). Include a way for people to identify themselves as male or female. Distribute the forms to each member of your sample. Collect the completed forms.

Step 4: Analyze data. List your 4 choices in the first column of the table below. Divide the surveys into those submitted by males and those submitted by females. Add the scores for the first choice from all males. Write this total in the first cell below *Males.* Add the scores for the second choice from all males. Write this total in the second cell under *Males.* After you complete the column for males, add scores for the *Females* column. Complete the *Total Score* column by totaling the scores across rows.

Which choice received the highest total score?

_____

What fraction of this total score came from males?

_____

What fraction of this total score came from females?

_____

Popularity of _____			
Choices	**Males**	**Females**	**Total Score**

Step 5: Interpret results. Write a one–sentence answer to your study question.

_____

_____

Lesson 3.3 Sampling

When a **population**, or data set, has a very large number of data points, sampling can be used to help summarize the data set.

Representative samples can be obtained from a population by choosing members at random. **Random sampling** selects members from a population in a way so that each member has an equal chance of being chosen. If members are not selected in a fair way, the sampling is **biased**. Biased samples will not produce an accurate representation of the population.

Diana is trying to find out what kind of music 7th graders prefer. If she was to interview the first 60 seventh graders to arrive at school one morning, she would be using random sampling because school arrival time has nothing to do with taste in music. If she was to interview 60 7th graders who are taking band, or who are at a concert for a specific band, she would be using biased sampling because both of those factors can affect someone's taste in music.

Tell if each sample would be considered *random* or *biased*.

1. Charlie puts a deck of cards in a bag. He shakes the bag and pulls 4 cards out of the bag.

   _____

2. Nicole wanted to know what 6th graders' favorite movie of the year was. She asked 10 girls from her homeroom class.

   _____

3. A garden has 100 pepper plants. John wants to know the number of peppers that are on each of the plants. He counts the number of peppers on the plants in one of the outside rows.

   _____

4. Ben wants to know what time most 7th graders get on the bus in the morning. He surveys five students from each bus.

   _____

5. Anna wants to know how much middle school students weigh. She weighs 1 student from each homeroom.

   _____

6. Jordan wants to know which restaurant makes the best burger in town. He stands on a block between two different burger restaurants at dinner time and asks the first 25 people that walk by.

   _____

Lesson 3.3 Sampling

When sampling a data set, there are several approaches that can be used to create a random sample.

Types of Random Samples	
Simple Random Sample	Members of a data set are randomly selected so that every member has an equal chance of being selected.
Stratified Random Sample	The data set is divided into similar groups that do not overlap. Then, a sample is chosen from each group.
Systematic Random Sample	The sample is chosen starting from a specific point and continuing for a chosen interval.

There are also different ways of creating a biased sample.

Types of Biased Samples	
Convenience Sample	The sample is made up of data points that are easy to access instead of making an effort to gather a larger, more diverse sample.
Voluntary Response Sample	The data set is made up information from people who volunteered to participate. Volunteers are often biased toward one outcome.

Name the type of sampling used in each situation.

1. At a factory, every 100th piece of candy is taken off the assembly line to be inspected.

    _____

2. A reporter for the school newspaper asks 10 students in the cafeteria who would make the best student council president.

    _____

3. Your math teacher calls on every 3rd name alphabetically to answer questions.

    _____

4. Fifteen students from your school get to represent your school at a news conference. Everybody's names are put in a box by grade level and 5 names are drawn from each box.

    _____

5. Shana announces to her class that she wants to know which new movie is their favorite. She calls on the first 10 people to raise their hands.

    _____

Lesson 3.4 Drawing Inferences from Data

Data sets from random samples can be used to make inferences about the data from the population.

Billy is collecting information on how long his classmates spend studying each week. He talks to 11 different students from his class of 29 and collects the information show on the histogram below.

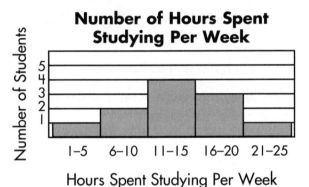

Number of Hours Spent Studying Per Week

Number of Students / Hours Spent Studying Per Week

The following information can be determined using this data:

- 4 students spend 11–15 hours each week studying.
- 4 out of 11 is 36.36% of the sample.
- 36.36% of 29 is 10.54.
- This means that it is most likely that 10 or 11 students in Billy's class spend 11–15 hours each week studying.

Use the data below to make inferences and answer the questions.

This histogram shows the test scores from a sample of 30 students. There are 125 students in the 7th grade.

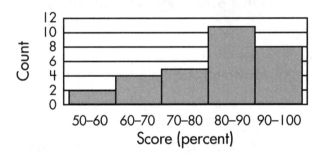

Test Scores of Students

Count / Score (percent)

1. How many students from the sample scored between 70 and 80 on the test?

   _____

2. What percentage of students from the sample scored between 70 and 80 on the test?

   _____

3. Predict how many students in the 7th grade scored between 70 and 80 on the test.

   _____

4. What percentage of students from the sample scored between 90 and 100 on the test?

   _____

5. Based on the percentage of students from the sample who scored between 90 and 100 on the test, how many students in 7th grade scored between 90 and 100?

   _____

6. If there were 150 students in 7th grade, how many students would have scored between 60 and 70 on the test?

   _____

Lesson 3.4 Drawing Inferences from Data

The coach of the Wilson High School baseball team is collecting information about how well his pitchers are performing. He keeps data about every third game.

	Walks	Hits	Strikeouts
Game 3	2	1	4
Game 6	1	2	3
Game 9	0	1	4
Game 12	0	4	6
Game 15	3	5	1
Game 18	3	4	2
Game 21	2	6	4
Game 24	4	5	6
Game 27	2	4	4
Game 30	1	4	2

The following information can be inferred using this data:

• Pitchers struck out 4 hitters in 4 games from the sample.

• 40% of the sample games had 4 strikeouts.

• It is most likely that there were 4 strikeouts in about 12 of the 30 games.

Use the data above to answer the questions.

1. What percentage of the sample games had no walks?

   _____

2. How many total hits were given up in the sample?

   _____

3. What would be a realistic prediction about the number of total hits in 30 games?

   _____

4. How many games out of the 30 games were most likely to have had 5 or more hits?

   _____

5. What percentage of the sample games had 2 walks?

   _____

6. What would be a realistic prediction about the number of total games that had 2 walks?

   _____

Lesson 3.4 Drawing Inferences from Data

Dawn is trying to find out how many brothers and sisters teachers in her school have. There are 54 teachers at the school, and she talks to 18 teachers. This is the data she collects: 1, 1, 1, 2, 0, 1, 2, 0, 1, 2, 4, 0, 1, 2, 3, 4, 5, 9.

This is the information that can be inferred about the data Dawn collected:

- 2 out of the 18 teachers sampled have 4 siblings.

- 11.11% of the teachers sampled have 4 siblings.

- It is most likely that 5 or 6 teachers at the school have 4 siblings.

Use the data below to answer the questions.

Mrs. Jones is giving a science test and she is trying to make sure students are spending enough time studying for the test. She chooses 5 students from each of her four classes and asks how many hours they spent studying. She collects the following information: $\frac{1}{2}$, $1\frac{1}{2}$, 3, 1, 2, $3\frac{1}{2}$, 1, $1\frac{1}{2}$, $1\frac{1}{2}$, 2, $3\frac{1}{2}$, 2, $1\frac{1}{2}$, 2, 2, $3\frac{1}{2}$, $2\frac{1}{2}$, $1\frac{1}{2}$, $3\frac{1}{2}$, 3.

1. How many students were included in Mrs. Jones's sample?

   _____

2. If she has 25 students in each class, how many students are in her population?

   _____

3. What percentage of the sample spent 2 hours studying for the test?

   _____

4. Based on this sample, about how many students from all of the classes spent 2 hours studying for the test?

   _____

5. Based on this sample, about how many students from all of the classes spent at least $2\frac{1}{2}$ hours studying for the test?

   _____

6. Based on this sample, about how many students from all of the classes spent less than 2 hours studying for the test?

   _____

Check What You Learned

Statistical Thinking

Read each question and write *statistical* or *not statistical.*

1. How many classes do I take in a day? _____

2. What are my classmates' favorite types of candy? _____

3. What color pants were worn by a boy at school today? _____

4. What is the region of the country with the lowest winter temperature? _____

Tell if each sample would be considered *random* or *biased.*

a	b
5. 10 students' heights are measured	every student's time of arrival at school is recorded
_____	_____
6. every 5th water bottle is checked	a teacher records all students' test grades
_____	_____

Solve the problems.

7. A survey of student drivers found that 77 out of 350 of them drive late at night. How many students in the next group of 100 surveyed would be expected to drive late at night?

   _____

8. An editor finds errors in the last 30 out of 100 articles submitted by a writer. In how many of the next 10 articles would you expect the editor to find no errors?

   _____

9. A student has flipped a coin and guessed heads or tails correctly 30 out of 40 coin flips. What is the experimental probability that the student will guess the next flip wrong?

   _____

Mid-Test Chapters 1–3

Determine the probabilities in each situation. Express each probability as a fraction in simplest form.

1. A jar contains 7 red, 2 white, and 6 blue marbles. If a marble is randomly selected, what is the probability of selecting the following colored marbles?

   a. red marble _____

   b. white marble _____

   c. blue marble _____

   d. not a red marble _____

2. You flip a coin that has a heads side and a tails side. What is the probability it does not land on heads?

   _____

3. A 6-sided die is rolled twice. What is the probability of rolling the following?

   a. two even numbers _____

   b. 1 and 6 _____

4. A die is rolled and a coin is tossed. Find the following probabilities.

   a. 1 and a head _____

   b. an even number and a head _____

   c. an odd number and a tail _____

5. A die is rolled 30 times. The results are shown in the table.

   What is the experimental probability of rolling the following?

   a. an even number _____

   b. an odd number _____

   c. 6 _____

Result	Frequency
1	4
2	6
3	2
4	8
5	3
6	7

6. A spinner has four equal sections numbered from 1 to 4. What is the probability of spinning the following?

   a. 1 _____

   b. an even number _____

7. A dart board has 20 equal sections numbered 1 through 20. If a dart is thrown at the board, what is the probability of it landing on the following?

   a. an even number _____

   b. a number greater than 11 _____

   c. a multiple of 2 _____

Write *yes* or *no* to tell if each situation describes uniform probability.

8. a 4-part spinner with 2 red parts, 1 white part, and 1 yellow part _____

9. flipping a coin with a heads side and a tails side _____

10. randomly selecting a fruit from a bin with 5 oranges, 3 apples, and 2 bananas in it

   _____

11. selecting a letter from the name "Johnny" _____

Solve the problems.

12. Computers in an assembly line were tested. The test determined that 5 out of 1,000 were

   defective. What is the probability that a computer tested is not defective? _____

13. In a survey of 1,000 students, 235 students were found to study math and English together.
   Based on these results, in a new survey of 1,200 students, how many students would be

   expected to study math and English together? _____

14. A cabinet contains 4 red mugs, 3 blue mugs, and 2 yellow mugs. What is the probability of

   randomly selecting a blue or yellow mug? _____

15. A quarter is flipped and a die is rolled.

   a. How many possible outcomes are there? _____

   b. How can this situation be simulated? _____

   _____

   c. What is the probability of getting heads and a 6? _____

16. A test has 3 true-false questions on it.
   Use a tree diagram to show all of the
   possible combinations of answers to the test.

Mid-Test Chapters 1–3

Solve the problems.

17. Thomas has two spinners each with equal sections. The first spinner has 4 colors: red, orange, blue, and green. The second spinner has numbers 1 through 5. What is the probability of spinning red and the number 4?

_____

18. Three dice are rolled. What is the probability of rolling 3 fives?

_____

19. A spinner with equal sections numbered 1 through 10 is spun twice. What is the probability that the first spin lands on a 3 and the second spin lands on a 3?

_____

20. How many 3-letter passwords are there that consist only of letters if each letter cannot be repeated?

_____

Read each question and write *statistical* or *not statistical*.

21. **a.** What fraction of students in your class has dinner between 5:00 and 6:00 P.M.? _____

 b. Which students are taller than 6 feet? _____

 c. How much does this computer cost? _____

 d. What color is the car? _____

 e. Which is the most liked fruit of 5-year-old children? _____

 f. How many home runs will this player hit tonight? _____

 g. How fast does this motorcycle go? _____

 h. How many pages does your notebook have? _____

 i. What is the average time spent on homework? _____

 j. How many calories are in this meal? _____

Mid-Test Chapters 1–3

Tell if each sample would be considered *random* or *biased*.

22. All students on one school bus are surveyed to find out how many middle school students bring their lunch.

_____

23. Every 5th cell phone in a batch from an assembly line is checked to find the percentage of defective cell phones.

_____

24. All customers entering a grocery store are asked if there is a new coupon system being used in the store.

_____

25. The entire 7th grade in a school is surveyed to vote on the most popular student in a class.

_____

26. To determine what products are most popular, a store surveys a small group of customers at each of its stores.

_____

Solve the problems.

27. A spinner has a triangle, square, and circle on three equal sections. If it were spun 300 times, how many times would it be expected to land on a circle?

_____

28. A principal surveys 750 students in his school about their music preference and finds that 35% prefer rock music. How many students out of 1,500 would be expected to prefer rock music?

_____

29. A company produces 5 defective water bottles out of 5,000 for a batch run. What is the probability of the next bottle being defective?

_____

Check What You Know

Measures of Central Tendency and Measures of Variability

Find the mean, median, mode, and range of each set of data. Round to the nearest tenth.

a

1. 8, 9, 4, 2, 9

mean: _____

median: _____

mode: _____

range: _____

b

25, 17, 14, 29, 17, 24

mean: _____

median: _____

mode: _____

range: _____

c

6, 4, 0, 2, 5, 7, 1, 3

mean: _____

median: _____

mode: _____

range: _____

2. Dana scored 80, 86, 79, and 81 on her first 4 math quizzes. What score does she need on the fifth quiz to reach an average of 84?

a. Equation: _____ **b.** Dana needs a score of _____.

3. Kerry's Berries sold a mean of 24 quarts of blueberries per day. The store sold a total of 720 quarts during the sample period. How many days are in the sample?

a. Equation: _____ **b.** The sample has _____ days.

The stem-and-leaf plot represents a set of data. Use the plot to answer the questions.

4. Which numbers in the set are in the

   30–39 interval? _____

5. What is the mode of the set? _____

6. What is the median of the set? _____

7. What is the lowest number in the set? _____

8. What is the range of the set? _____

Stem	Leaves
2	1 4
3	2 5 7
4	1 3 4 9
5	6 6 8
6	1 1 1

Key: 2 | 4 = 24

NAME _____

Check What You Know

Measures of Central Tendency and Measures of Variability

9. A car dealer surveyed customers to find out which car color they prefer. Survey responses are shown in the frequency table. Complete the table. Round to tenths.

Popularity of Colors for Cars			
Color	Frequency	Cumulative Frequency	Relative Frequency
red	25		%
blue	20		%
black	16		%
silver	43		%
white	36		%

10. How many customers responded to the survey? _____

11. What color was most popular? _____

12. What percentage of customers preferred blue or white? _____%

Use the line plot to answer the questions.

13. What is the mode? _____

14. What is the range? _____

15. How many years does the plot include? _____

16. What is the median? _____

Tornadoes per Year in a State

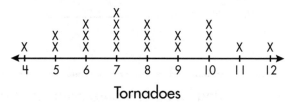

Tornadoes

Use the box-and-whisker plot to answer the questions.

17. What is the median? _____

18. What is the upper quartile? _____

19. What is the interquartile range? _____

Number of Movies Watched over Summer

Movies

Lesson 4.1 Measures of Central Tendency

Mean, median, and mode are measures of central tendency. You can use these measures to analyze sets of data.

The **mean** is the average of a set of numbers. To find the mean, add all the numbers in the set and divide by the number of addends.

The **median** is the middle number of a set of numbers. If the set contains an even number of values, the median is the mean, or average, of the two middle numbers.

The **mode** is the most frequent number—the number that appears most often in a set of numbers. A set can have no mode, one mode, or more than one mode. If all the numbers in a set occur the same number of times, the set has no mode. If two or more numbers appear most often, then each of those numbers is a mode of that set.

Find the mean of the set 12, 15, 18, 23, 8, 10, 12.

mean: $12 + 15 + 18 + 23 + 8 + 10 + 12 = 98$ $\frac{98}{7} = 14$

To find the median and mode, arrange the numbers in order: 8, 10, 12, 12, 15, 18, 23

median: 12   mode: 12

Find the median of 8, 6, 5, 7, 2, 10. First, order the numbers: 2, 5, 6, 7, 8, 10

The middle numbers are 6 and 7. median: $\frac{6+7}{2} = \frac{13}{2} = 6\frac{1}{2}$

Find the mean, median, and mode of each set of numbers.

	a	**b**
1.	25, 20, 14, 25, 16	32, 36, 21, 19, 21, 36
	mean: _____	mean: _____
	median: _____	median: _____
	mode: _____	mode: _____
2.	23, 8, 2, 11, 65, 6, 4	5, 13, 0, 45, 80, 0, 5, 0
	mean: _____	mean: _____
	median: _____	median: _____
	mode: _____	mode: _____

Lesson 4.1 Measures of Central Tendency

Another way to examine a set of data is to look at how spread out the data is. Range is a measure of spread. The **range** of a set of numbers is the difference between the greatest and least numbers in the set.

Find the mean and range of these sets of data.

Set A: 60, 64, 59, 57, 60

order the numbers: 57, 59, 60, 60, 64

range: $64 - 57 = 7$

mean: $\frac{300}{5} = 60$

Set B: 52, 35, 75, 110, 28

order the numbers: 28, 35, 52, 75, 110

range: $110 - 28 = 82$

mean: $\frac{300}{5} = 60$

Both sets of data have a mean of 60. However, Set B has a larger range than Set A. The larger range means that the data are more spread out in Set B than in Set A.

The following table lists test scores for 3 students. Use the table to answer the questions.

Student	Test 1	Test 2	Test 3	Test 4	Test 5
Cory	88	93	81	97	84
Kara	85	84	84	86	83
Suki	90	92	88	85	92

1. Write Cory's scores in order: _____

   Cory's mean: _____ median: _____ mode: _____ range: _____

2. Write Kara's scores in order: _____

   Kara's mean: _____ median: _____ mode: _____ range: _____

3. Write Suki's scores in order: _____

   Suki's mean: _____ median: _____ mode: _____ range: _____

4. Which student performed most consistently on the tests? Explain your answer.

_____

Lesson 4.1 Measures of Central Tendency

Each measure of central tendency provides a useful, but different, way to analyze sets of data. The mean evens out, or balances, a set of data. The mean is a good way to describe the middle of a set of data that does not have an outlier. An **outlier** is an extreme value, a number that is much larger or smaller than the other numbers in the set.

The median is a good way to describe the middle of a set that does have an outlier. An outlier affects the median less than the mean. The mode is useful for data that are not numbers. For example, you might use the mode to identify the most popular item in a set.

Consider this ordered set: 9, 9, 10, 10, 14, 35   mean = 87 ÷ 6 = 14.5   median = 10

The number 35 is much higher than the other numbers. What if we remove the outlier?

Set with outlier removed: 9, 9, 10, 10, 14   mean = 52 ÷ 5 = 10.4   median = 10

Without the outlier, the mean declined significantly, but the median was not affected.

The hourly wages of employees at two stores are shown below. Use measures of central tendency to analyze the data. Round to the nearest cent.

	a **Sam's Pet World**	**b** **Beth's Pets**
Hourly wages ($)	10, 9.5, 8.25, 9, 10, 9.5, 8.5, 10.5	9.25, 8, 7.5, 8.5, 7.75, 20, 8, 9
1. mean	$_____	$_____
2. median	$_____	$_____
3. mode	$_____	$_____

4. Which store do you think pays its employees better? Explain your answer.

_____

_____

5. Suppose you are Beth. You want to convince a potential employee that you pay your employees well. What measure of central tendency would you use? Why?

_____

_____

NAME _____

Lesson 4.1   Measures of Central Tendency

Sometimes, you may know the mean and need to find a missing piece of data. You can use equations to solve for the missing number.

Midori has these scores on three math tests: 88, 92, 94. Midori wants to know what score she needs on the fourth test to bring her average up to 92.

Mean: $\quad \frac{88 + 92 + 94 + n}{4} = 92$ $n =$ the score on the fourth test

$\qquad\qquad \frac{274 + n}{4} = 92$ simplify

$\qquad\qquad 274 + n = 368$ multiply each side by 4

$\qquad\qquad\qquad n = 94$ subtract 274 from each side

Midori must get a 94 on the fourth test to bring her average up to 92.

Use an equation to find the missing number in each problem. Show your work.

1. In six basketball games, Diego scored 14, 16, 11, 18, 12, and 17 points. By the end of the next game, Diego wants his average to be 15 points per game. How many points must Diego score in the seventh game to achieve his goal?

   Diego must score _____ points.

2. The mean temperature in an area is 74 degrees Fahrenheit. The sum of the temperatures is 2,516. How many temperatures are in the set?

   There are _____ temperatures in the set.

3. The mean of 25 prices is $11.40. What is the sum of the set of prices?

   The sum of the set is $ _____ .

Spectrum Data Analysis and Probability
Grades 6–8
56

Lesson 4.1
Measures of Central Tendency and Measures of Variability

Lesson 4.2 Measures of Variability: Range

The **range** of a data set is the difference between the largest value and smallest value contained in the data set.

	11, 12, 15, 15, 13, 12
Step 1: Put the data set in order from least to greatest.	11, 12, 12, 13, 15, 15
Step 2: Find the largest value and smallest value.	<u>11</u>, 12, 12, 13, 15, <u>15</u>
Step 3: Subtract.	15 − 11 =
Step 4: The range of this data set is 4.	4

Find the range of each data set.

          a   **b**

1. 11, 10, 12, 9   79, 79, 79, 84

   _____   _____

2. 25, 30, 32, 23, 27, 22   96, 94, 101, 96, 91, 92

   _____   _____

3. 36, 33, 37, 37, 41, 33   506, 508, 510, 509

   _____   _____

4. 277, 280, 287, 276   68, 66, 59, 54, 61

   _____   _____

5. 12, 9, 16, 9   95, 92, 89, 97, 94, 88

   _____   _____

Lesson 4.3 Measures of Variability: Interquartile Range

The **interquartile range** (IQR) of a data set is the difference between the median of the lower half of a data set and the median of the upper half of the same data set.

	13, 15, 9, 35, 25, 17, 19
Step 1: Put the data set in order from least to greatest.	9, 13, 15, 17, 19, 25, 35
Step 2: Find the lower half, median, and upper half of the data set.	9, 13, 15 17 19, 25, 35
Step 3: Find the medians of the lower half and upper half.	Q1 = 13 Q3 = 25
Step 4: Subtract.	25 − 13 =
Step 5: The interquartile range of the data set is 12.	12

Find the interquartile range for each set of data.

a	b

1. 6, 1, 3, 8, 5, 11, 1, 5   80, 90, 95, 85, 70

   median: _____   median: _____

   Q1: _____   Q1: _____

   Q3: _____   Q3: _____

   IQR: _____   IQR: _____

2. 70, 75, 90, 100, 95   45, 43, 13, 11, 5, 2

   median: _____   median: _____

   Q1: _____   Q1: _____

   Q3: _____   Q3: _____

   IQR: _____   IQR: _____

3. 45, 39, 17, 16, 4, 1   29, 58, 15, 75, 22, 16, 64

   median: _____   median: _____

   Q1: _____   Q1: _____

   Q3: _____   Q3: _____

   IQR: _____   IQR: _____

NAME _____

Lesson 4.4 Measures of Variability: Mean Absolute Deviation

The **mean absolute deviation** (MAD) of a data set is a value that shows if the data set is consistent. The closer the mean absolute deviation of a data set to zero, the more consistent it is.

	17, 19, 8, 32, 21, 24, 19
Step 1: Put the data set in order from least to greatest.	8, 17, 19, 19, 21, 24, 32
Step 2: Find the mean of the data set.	Mean = 20
Step 3: Find the absolute value of the difference between the mean and each value in the set. (For example, $20 - 8 = 12$; $|12| = 12$)	12, 3, 1, 1, 1, 4, 12
Step 4: Find the mean of those absolute values.	Mean = 8.71
Step 5: The mean absolute deviation of this data set is 8.71. This tells us that the values in the set are on average about 8.71 away from the middle.	MAD = 8.71

Find the mean absolute deviation of each data set. Round each answer to two decimal places.

a

1. 10, 16, 18, 15, 15, 10, 23

mean: _____

value differences:

_____

MAD: _____

2. 10, 12, 18, 25, 25, 11, 22

mean: _____

value differences:

_____

MAD: _____

b

41, 56, 38, 45, 55, 51, 52

mean: _____

value differences:

_____

MAD: _____

22, 33, 44, 55, 66, 88, 55, 55, 11, 22

mean: _____

value differences:

_____

MAD: _____

Lesson 4.5 Using Measures of Variability

The **range** of a data set is the difference between the largest value and smallest value contained in the data set.

The **interquartile range** (IQR) of a data set is the difference between the median of the lower half of a data set and the median of the upper half of the same data set.

The **mean absolute deviation** (MAD) of a data set is a value that helps understand if the data set is consistent. If the mean absolute deviation of a data set is close to zero, the data set is more consistent.

Complete the table by listing the measures of variability for each data set. Round answers to two decimal places.

Data	Range	IQR	MAD
1. 43, 48, 80, 53, 59, 65, 58, 66, 70, 50, 76, 62	_____	_____	_____
2. 12, 47, 26, 25, 38, 45, 35, 35, 41, 39, 32, 25, 18, 30	_____	_____	_____
3. 99, 45, 23, 67, 45, 91, 82, 78, 62, 51	_____	_____	_____
4. 10, 2, 5, 6, 7, 3, 4	_____	_____	_____
5. 23, 56, 45, 65, 59, 55, 61, 54, 85, 25	_____	_____	_____
6. 55, 63, 88, 97, 58, 90, 88, 71, 65, 77, 75, 88, 95, 86	_____	_____	_____

Lesson 4.6 Frequency Tables

Frequency is the number of times a value occurs in a data set. **Cumulative frequency** is the sum of all frequencies up to and including the current one. **Relative frequency** is frequency expressed as a percent or fraction of the total.

To make a frequency table for these test scores:

71, 85, 73, 92, 86, 79, 87, 98, 82, 93, 81, 89, 88, 96

Step 1: Order the scores: 71, 73, 79, 81, 82, 85, 86, 87, 88, 89, 92, 93, 96, 98

Step 2: Make reasonable intervals. Here, intervals are 5 points.

Step 3: Sum the frequencies in each interval for the Frequency column.

Step 4: Calculate cumulative frequencies by adding the frequency of each interval to the previous total.

Test Scores			
Score	Frequency	Cumulative Frequency	Relative Frequency
71–75	2	2	14.3%
76–80	1	3	7.1%
81–85	3	6	21.4%
86–90	4	10	28.6%
91–95	2	12	14.3%
96–100	2	14	14.3%

Step 5: Calculate relative frequencies as percents or fractions of the total items in the set, which is the last cumulative frequency.

Complete the frequency table. Calculate relative frequencies as fractions in simplest form and as percents rounded to the nearest tenth. Then, answer the questions.

Pet Ownership				
Number of Pets	Frequency	Cumulative Frequency	Relative Frequency (fraction)	Relative Frequency (percent)
0	8	8		%
1	29	37		%
2	15	52		%
3	6	58		%
4+	2	60		%

1. How many people were polled? _____

2. What fraction of the people polled have 2 or 3 pets? _____

Lesson 4.6 Frequency Tables

Fill in the missing numbers in the frequency table. Then, answer the questions.

Points Scored per Basketball Game			
Points	Frequency	Cumulative Frequency	Relative Frequency
30–39		3	$\frac{1}{10}$
40–49		8	
50–59		16	
60–69		26	
70–79		30	

1. How many games does this data cover? _____

2. How many points are in each interval? _____

Use the following data to complete the frequency table and answer the questions.

Heights of students in a class, in feet: 5.2, 5.6, 4.6, 6.0, 5.4, 5.1, 4.6, 5.2, 5.9, 6.1, 5.5, 5.2, 5.8, 5.3, 5.6, 5.9, 5.4, 5.7, 5.4, 4.8.

3. Arrange the heights in order, from shortest to tallest: _____

_____

Heights of Students in a Class			
Height, in Feet	Frequency	Cumulative Frequency	Relative Frequency
4.5–4.9			%
5.0–5.4			%
5.5–5.9			%
6.0–6.5			%

4. How many students are in the class? _____

5. The heights of most of the students fall within what interval? _____ feet.

6. What percent of the students are 6 feet tall or taller? _____%

7. What percent of the students are less than 6 feet tall? _____%

Lesson 4.7 Stem-and-Leaf Plots

A **stem-and-leaf plot** is a way to organize data to examine the shape. Stem-and-leaf plots display the data in two columns, using place values. The right column shows the **leaves**—the "ones" digit of each number. The other digits are the **stems**, which appear in the left column. The key explains how to read the plot.

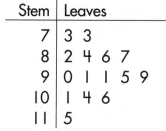

Use the following data to create a stem-and-leaf plot:

82, 95, 115, 84, 91, 87, 90, 104, 86, 91, 73, 99, 101, 73, 106

Step 1: Arrange the numbers in order, from least to greatest. 73, 73, 82, 84, 86, 87, 90, 91, 91, 95, 99, 101, 104, 106, 115

Step 2: Make a vertical list of stems, from the lowest "tens" digit to the highest digit. Use a vertical line to separate the stem and leaves.

Step 3: List each "ones" digit next to its stem.

Step 4: Add a key that tells how to read the plot.

The lengths of the leaves give you a sense of the shape and spread of the data. To see these characteristics, visualize the plot turned sideways, as shown at right. The data have been enclosed in bars to help you visualize. The height of each leaf column shows the shape of the data.

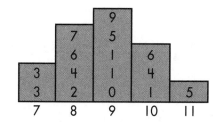

Use the stem-and-leaf plot above to answer these questions.

1. What is the mode of this data? _____

2. What is the highest number in this data set? _____

3. What is the lowest number in this data set? _____

4. What is the range? _____

Lesson 4.7 Stem-and-Leaf Plots

Unlike frequency tables, stem-and-leaf plots keep the raw data. For example, a frequency table might show that 3 numbers in the set fall in the 30–39 interval. However, the table does not tell you the exact numbers. A stem-and-leaf plot gives the numbers:

Stem	Leaves
3	4 8

The numbers in the 30–39 range are 34 and 38.

Create a stem-and-leaf plot and key for each set of data. Then, answer the questions.

1. 46, 29, 35, 44, 29, 26, 55, 46, 53, 27, 32, 31, 22

Stem	Leaves

Key: _____

2. 441, 432, 455, 435, 469, 451, 442, 469, 451, 443, 455

Stem	Leaves

Key: _____

3. Chicago, Illinois posted the following high temperatures (in degrees Fahrenheit) for the month of April: 83, 81, 59, 76, 72, 76, 49, 40, 56, 74, 63, 70, 63, 80, 82, 68, 59, 52, 56, 64, 62, 60, 63, 60, 60, 63, 46, 59, 70, 74

Stem	Leaves

Key: _____

4. What was the mode for Chicago in April? _____ degrees

5. What was the range of high temperatures for the month? _____ degrees

6. What temperature was the median for the month? _____ degrees

Lesson 4.8 Line Plots

A **line plot** is a graph that shows frequency of data on a number line. Line plots make it easy to identify the mode, range, and any outliers. Recall that an outlier is an extreme value, a number that is much larger or smaller than the other numbers in the set.

To make a line plot, draw a number line from the least to the greatest value in the number set. Then, make an X above each number every time it appears in the set. The number of Xs above each number shows how many times that number appears—its frequency.

Height of My Classmates

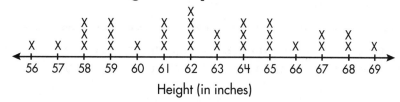

Height (in inches)

What is the mode, or most frequent height? Look for the tallest stack of Xs. The mode is 62 inches. What is the range of heights in the class? Subtract the least height from the greatest: 69 − 56 = 13 inches. How many students were polled? Count the total number of Xs. Thirty students were polled. What is the median height of the students? Count 15 Xs in from the left and 15 Xs in from the right. The median is the average of these two numbers. Because both numbers are 62 inches, the median is 62 inches.

The Eagles baseball team scored these numbers of runs per game: 4, 2, 6, 3, 1, 0, 2, 0, 4, 5, 0, 7, 6, 4, 3, 2, 6, 8, 1, 3, 11, 7, 3. Make a line plot. Then, answer the questions.

⟵————————————————————————⟶

1. What is the mode? _____ What is the range? _____

2. How many games did the Eagles play? _____ What is the median? _____

3. If there is an outlier, identify it. _____

Lesson 4.8 Line Plots

Line plots can also help you see clusters and gaps in the data. Clusters are groups of points separated from other points. Gaps are large spaces between points.

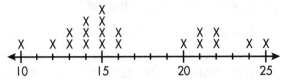

The largest clusters of data in the plot lie in the 12 through 16 range and the 20 through 22 range. The largest gap is 17 through 19.

As a store manager, you collected data on the average number of transactions that each sales clerk handled in a day. Use the plot of the data below to answer the questions.

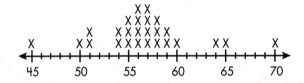

1. What is the mode? _____

2. What is the data range? _____

3. How many sales clerks does the store employ? _____

4. What is the median number of transactions? _____

5. Based on the data, what range of transactions would you consider a standard day's work for a sales clerk? Explain why.

_____

6. Above what number of transactions would you consider giving an award for employee of the month? Explain your reasoning.

_____

Lesson 4.9 Box-and-Whisker Plots

A **box-and-whisker plot** displays data along a number line, using quartiles. Quartiles are numbers that divide the data into quarters, or 4 equal parts. The median, or middle quartile, divides the data in half. The lower quartile is the median of the lower half of the data. The upper quartile is the median of the upper half of the data.

Twenty-five percent of the data lies between quartiles. The upper and lower quartiles, enclosing 50% of the data, form the box. The upper extreme (highest value) and lower extreme (lowest value) form the whiskers.

To draw a box-and-whisker plot, first arrange the data in order:

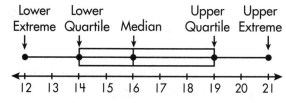

12, 13, 14, 14, 15, 16, 17, 18, 19, 19, 21

Middle Quartile (median): 16
Upper Extreme: 21   Upper Quartile (median of upper half): 19
Lower Extreme: 12   Lower Quartile (median of lower half): 14

Use the box-and-whisker plot below to answer the following questions.

1. The most miles ridden were _____ .

2. The fewest miles ridden were _____ .

Miles Ridden in a Bike-a-Thon

3. Half the riders rode _____ miles or more.

4. If 80 riders participated, how many people rode 40–45 miles? _____

The scores on a quiz were 5, 10, 15, 25, 30, 35, 40.

5. What is the median of these scores? _____

6. What is the lower quartile? _____   What is the upper quartile? _____

7. Using the number line below, draw a box-and-whisker plot for these scores.

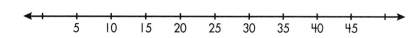

Lesson 4.9   Box-and-Whisker Plots

A box-and-whisker plot does not show the number of data points. As a result, you cannot use this kind of plot to find the mean or mode. A box-and-whisker plot helps you see at a glance the center, the spread, and the overall range of the data.

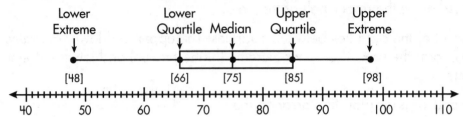

To find the range of the set, subtract the lower extreme from the upper extreme: 98 − 48 = 50. The **interquartile range** is the range of the middle 50% of the data. To find the interquartile range, subtract the lower quartile from the upper quartile: 85 − 66 = 19.

Use the box-and-whiskers plots below to answer the questions.

1. The range of wages is _____.

2. The interquartile range is _____

3. The pay for the top 50% of workers ranges

   from $ _____ to _____.

Hourly Wages at XYZ Company

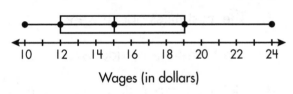

Wages (in dollars)

4. Are wages more spread out for the top 50% or bottom 50% of workers? _____

   How can you tell by looking at the plot? _____

   _____

5. The range of passengers is _____.

6. What range of passengers does the middle

   50% of flights carry? _____

Passengers per Flight from Airport X

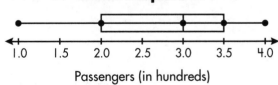

Passengers (in hundreds)

7. Is it likely that most planes that fly from Airport X can hold at least 300 passengers?

   Explain your answer _____

   _____

Lesson 4.10 Problem Solving

The table shows the weights of players on a football team, in pounds. Use this table to answer the questions. Round to the nearest pound.

1. How many players are on the football team? _____

2. What unit was used to measure the weight of the

   players on the team? _____

3. What is the mean? _____ pounds

4. What is the mode? _____ pounds

5. What is the median? _____ pounds

A player who weighs 150 pounds joined the team.

6. Now what is the mean? _____ pounds

7. What is the mode? _____ pounds

8. What is the median? _____ pounds

9. Which measure of central tendency was most influenced by the addition of an extreme value?

   _____

Team Roster	
Player	**Weight (lb.)**
Smith	250
Lawson	205
Stone	280
Reyes	200
Stein	280
Kwan	275
Turner	220
Rockwell	280
Koros	210
Manoa	300
Jones	250
Wilson	210

Suppose instead of a 150-pound player, the team added a 350-pound player to the roster.

10. What would happen to the mean? _____

11. What would happen to the mode? _____

12. What would happen to the median? _____

Suppose you are writing the media guide for the team shown in the table. You want to impress readers with how big your team is. Use the proper measurements to complete these statements for the guide:

13. "Half of our players weigh _____ pounds or more."

14. "We have more players who weigh _____ pounds than any other weight."

Lesson 4.10 Problem Solving

The box-and-whisker plots and the stem-and-leaf plots on this page compare the average high temperatures for Cleveland, Ohio, and Seattle, Washington, throughout the year. Use the plots to answer the questions.

Average High Temperature in Cleveland

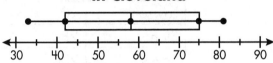

Average High Temperature in Seattle

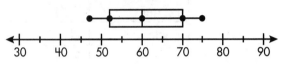

Average High Temperatures in °F (rounded)

Cleveland		Seattle
Leaves	Stem	Leaves
3 6 7	3	
6 9	4	7 7
7	5	1 2 5
1 9	6	0 0 5
2 7 9	7	0 0 5 5
1	8	

1. Which city has the mildest climate? _____

   a. How can you tell from the box-and-whisker plots?

   _____

   b. How can you tell from the stem-and-leaf plots?

   _____

2. Which city experiences the greatest seasonal temperature changes? _____

   a. How can you tell from the box-and-whisker plots?

   _____

   b. How can you tell from the stem-and leaf plots?

   _____

Compare the box-and-whisker and stem-and-leaf plots. Which would you use to compare:

3. the means? _____   4. the medians? _____

5. the modes? _____   6. the data spread? _____

Check What You Learned

Measures of Central Tendency

Find the mean, median, mode, and range of each set of data. Round to the nearest tenth.

	a	**b**	**c**
1.	22, 18, 3, 32, 18, 44	48, 15, 0, 23, 0, 2, 113	3, 12, 4, 3, 15, 4, 20, 12

mean: _____   mean: _____   mean: _____

median: _____   median: _____   median: _____

mode: _____   mode: _____   mode: _____

range: _____   range: _____   range: _____

2. Chris has these bowling scores: 130, 135, 129, 133. Then, she bowled a 165. Will this new score have the most effect on the mean, median, or mode? _____

3. Menendez Realty sold 24, 20, 26, 14, 18 houses each month. How many houses does the company need to sell to average 20 sales for the 6-month period?

   a. Equation: _____ **b.** The company must sell _____ houses.

4. The mean of 24 temperatures is 65°F. What is the sum of the set of temperatures?

   a. Equation: _____ **b.** The temperatures total _____°F.

5. Make a stem-and-leaf plot from this set of data: 236, 222, 267, 227, 239, 235, 251, 243, 256, 260, 244. Include a key. Use the plot to answer the questions.

6. What is the mode of the set? _____

7. What is the median of the set? _____

8. What is the lowest number in the set? _____

9. What is the range of the set? _____

Check What You Learned

Measures of Central Tendency

The times for the top finishers of a 10K race are, in minutes: 32, 34, 41, 35, 42, 46, 30, 44, 42, 34, 37, 44, 45, 44, 43. Use this data to answer the questions. Round to tenths.

10. Complete the frequency table.

Minutes	Frequency	Cumulative Frequency	Relative Frequency
30–34			%
35–39			%
40–44			%
45–49			%

11. Make a line plot to display this data.

12. Make a box-and-whisker plot for this data.

Find the following values from the data above.

	a		b
13.	mean: _____	range: _____
14.	median: _____	upper extreme: _____
15.	mode: _____	lower extreme: _____
16.	lower quartile: _____	interquartile range: _____

CHAPTER 4 POSTTEST

Check What You Know

Displaying Data

1. The sectors on the circle graph below were created from the data table. In the table, complete the percent and degrees columns. Then, complete the graph by including a graph title and sector labels. Match each country to the correct sector by measuring with a protractor, if necessary.

Annual Product Exports			
Country	Sales (millions)	%	Degrees
Germany	$12		
Great Britain	16		
France	10		
Canada	7		
China	4		
South Korea	1		
Total:	**$50**		

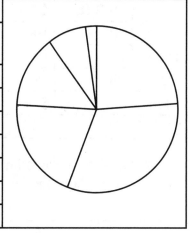

Refer to the graph to answer the following questions.

2. What does the graph show?

_____

_____

3. What interval is shown by each bar?

_____

4. Which age group has the greatest number of

investment dollars? _____

5. What information is shown on the frequency

axis in this histogram? _____

6. Which age category has $10.5 million in investments? _____

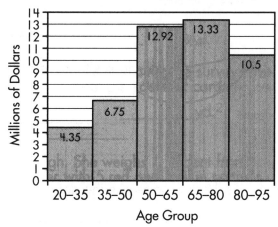

Trustworthy Investments, Inc.
Investments by Age Group

NAME _____

Check What You Know

Displaying Data

7. An animal shelter collected the data in the table below. Using the blank graph provided, create a multiple bar graph from the data table.

Animal Shelter Dog Adoptions			
	Under 20 lb.	20–50 lb.	Over 50 lb.
Oct.	18	14	12
Nov.	22	16	14
Dec.	28	19	18
Jan.	8	5	9
Feb.	17	18	4

8. What does the multiple line graph on the right show?

_____

_____

9. In which months did the shelter have more new arrivals than adoptions?

_____

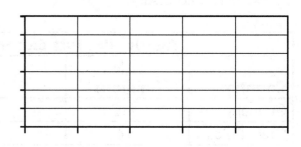

Animal Shelter New Arrivals and Adoptions, October-February

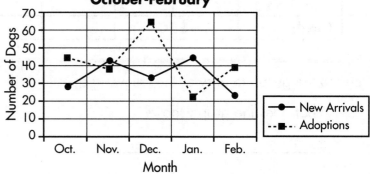

10. Describe the variables that are being compared in the scatter plot.

_____

_____

11. Is there a pattern in the data?

_____

12. Does the scatter plot show a positive correlation, a negative correlation, or no correlation?

_____

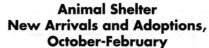

Age and Selling Price of Homes

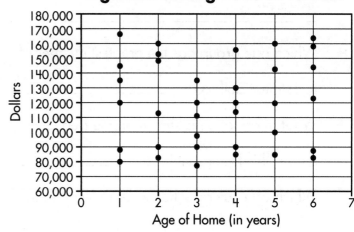

Lesson 5.1 Bar Graphs

A **bar graph** compares data collected from two or more sets of data. The vertical bar graph below was created from the sets of data shown in the table. A bar graph is intended to provide an overview of the data. The table presents the exact information.

There are two axes on a bar graph. The **group data axis** is at the base of the bars. In the graph below, the group data axis shows months. The **frequency axis** measures the frequency, or the amounts of the data. In the graph below, the frequency axis shows the units or number of bicycles sold. The scale on the frequency axis is determined by the range of the data. The data range is from 38 to 450. To contain this range, the scale runs from 0 to 500.

| Rick's Bike Shop ||
Month	Bicycles Sold
Jan.	40
Feb.	38
Mar.	110
Apr.	212
May	420
Jun.	450
Jul.	332
Aug.	313
Sep.	130
Oct.	109
Nov.	90
Dec.	340

Refer to the table and graph above to answer the following questions.

1. In which month did Rick's Bike Shop sell the most bikes? _____

   In which month did the shop sell the fewest bikes? _____

2. How many bikes did the shop sell from April through August? _____

   What percentage is this of total units sold for the year? _____

3. How many bikes did the shop sell from September through March? _____

   What percentage is this of total units sold for the year? _____

Lesson 5.1 Bar Graphs

A **multiple bar graph** allows you to compare two or more sets of data. The graph below shows three sets of data for each month. The graph was created from the data shown in the table.

Notice the key at the bottom of the graph. It identifies the data categories (the bars). This multiple bar graph appears in a horizontal format. It could also appear in a vertical format with the group data axis (the months) at the bottom of the graph and the frequency axis (the units) on the side of the graph.

Bicycle Sales by Price Category, May-August

Month	Over $400	$200–$399	Under $200	Totals
May	182	102	136	**420**
June	152	188	110	**450**
July	166	120	46	**332**
August	175	110	28	**313**
Totals	**675**	**520**	**320**	**1,515**

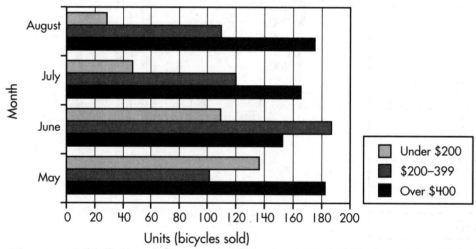

**Rick's Bike Shop
Bicycle Sales by Price Category**

Key:
- Under $200
- $200–399
- Over $400

Refer to the table and graph above to answer the following questions.

1. Which three categories of data are shown for each month?

   _____

2. **a.** Which category sold the most units from May through August? _____

   b. How many total units were sold in this category? _____

3. From May through August, what percentage of total units sold was under $200?

   _____

Lesson 5.2 Create a Bar Graph

You can use an electronic spreadsheet to create a bar graph or you can create it manually. Regardless of the method, the type of information you will provide for the graph is the same. Follow the steps below.

Phillips' Family Cars Miles Driven, April-Sept.			
Month	Subcompact	Full-Size Sedan	Pickup Truck
April	1,250	903	1,110
May	1,650	867	1,237
June	1,832	1,252	1,349
July	1,400	1,390	1,898
Aug.	1,280	1,367	1,278
Sept.	1,345	1,445	890

1 Make a table organizing the graph data.

2 Provide the scale for the frequency axis.

5 Provide a graph title.

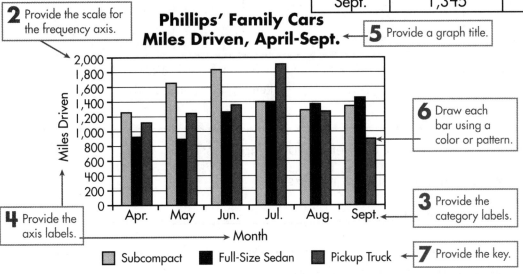

6 Draw each bar using a color or pattern.

3 Provide the category labels.

4 Provide the axis labels.

7 Provide the key.

Create a multiple bar graph on a separate piece of paper using the information in the table. Then, refer to the table and your graph to answer the questions.

1. What was George's total income in

   2007? _____ in 2011? _____

2. George's income from his full-time job increased steadily every year from 2007 to 2011. Why didn't his total income

   increase? _____

George Martin Sources of Income, 2007–2011			
Year	Full-time Job	Invest-ments	Part-time Job
2007	$22,745	$16,800	$5,222
2008	$23,288	$15,825	$5,005
2009	$24,366	$15,222	$4,789
2010	$25,456	$17,200	$2,200
2011	$28,972	$14,432	$1,200

NAME _____

Lesson 5.3 Histograms

A **histogram** is a type of bar graph. In a histogram, the categories are consecutive and the intervals are equal. Each bar shows a range of data. There is no space between the bars.

A histogram is created from a **frequency table**, as shown below.

An interval that does not have a frequency does not have a bar.

100 Meter Dash	
Running Times	**Frequency**
10.5–11	1
11–11.5	0
11.5–12.0	6
12.0–12.5	4
12.5–13.0	5

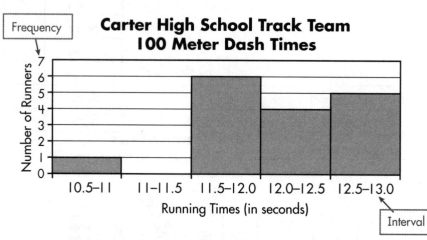

Refer to the table and histogram above to answer the following questions.

1. Which interval has the greatest number of runners? _____

2. Which interval does not have a frequency? _____

Refer to the histogram below to answer the following questions.

3. What information is shown on the frequency axis? _____

4. What do the intervals show? _____

5. How many employees drive 15 miles or less

   to work? _____

6. How many employees drive more than 15 miles

   to work? _____

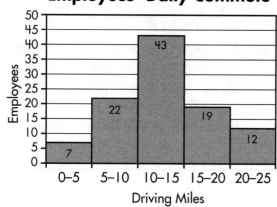

Lesson 5.4 Create a Histogram

Follow the steps below to create a histogram.

1. Data must be collected in a frequency table. List the data intervals (the Age Group column in the example below). Fill in the Frequency column.

Survey Respondents	
Age Group	**Frequency**
20–35	367
35–50	436
50–65	522
65–80	467
80–95	128

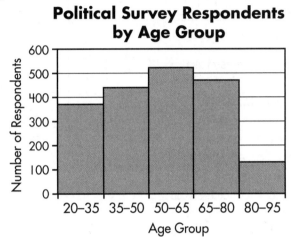

2. Draw and label the vertical and horizontal axes in your histogram. Provide a graph title.

3. Put the intervals on the horizontal axis and the frequencies on the vertical axis.

4. Draw in the bars. The intervals should be equal, so there should be no space between the bars. An interval with a frequency of 0 will have no bar.

Leland Outdoor Products must have enough service representatives to answer the phones during peak periods. A manager tracked the average number of customer calls for 3 months and put them in the frequency table below. Create a histogram on a separate piece of paper, and answer the following questions.

1. What information should go on the horizontal axis of your histogram? _____

the vertical axis? _____

2. The scale interval on the frequency axis would appear best in increments of: (circle one)

25   50   100   500

3. The manager needs additional staff to handle more than 300 calls in a time period. During which time periods might the manager need to add additional staff?

_____

Leland Outdoor Products	
Time Period	**Average Number of Calls**
8–10 am	172
10 am–12 pm	345
12–2 pm	290
2–4 pm	567
4–6 pm	580

Lesson 5.5 Line Graphs

A **line graph** shows how two variables relate to each other and how they change over time. The line graph at right shows the specific values at each data point.

A line graph shows data trends over time that may help you to make predictions. This could help to analyze or solve a problem. For example, Pelworth Technology School may need to look closely at enrollment data to adjust staffing for future enrollments.

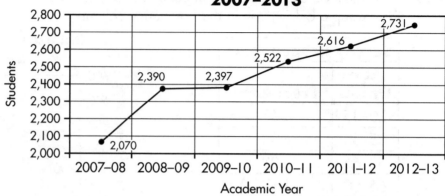

Pelworth Technology School Enrollment, 2007–2013

When analyzing data, you may need to calculate the percent of increase or decrease from one period to another. Remember that a percentage increase or decrease is in relation to the original value. Use the formula below:

$$\frac{\text{amount of increase or decrease}}{\text{original amount}} = \text{percent increase or decrease}$$

Refer to the line graph above to answer the following questions.

1. What information does the graph show during the time period? _____

2. What general trend does the graph show from the academic year

    2007–2008 to 2012–2013? _____

3. Which academic years do not follow this general trend? _____

4. Calculate the enrollment change from 2007–2008 to 2012–2013. Round your answer to the nearest whole percent.

    _____

5. Based on the percent of change you calculated in question 4, estimate the enrollment for the school in another 6 years.

    _____

Lesson 5.5 Line Graphs

A **multiple line graph** shows changes over a period of time in more than one category. This allows you to compare data.

For example, the line graph at right compares the sales of three different stores during the same period of time (January to June) of the current year.

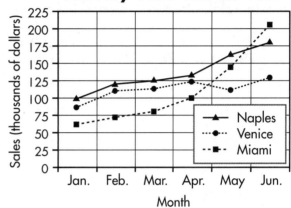

Thomas & Sons Boating Supplies Sales January–June Current Year

Refer to the graph above to answer the following questions.

1. Which store had the most consistent month-to-month sales? _____

2. Which store showed the greatest sales for a single month and the greatest overall change in

   sales from January to June? _____

Refer to the graph to answer the following questions.

3. In which weeks did each plant have the greatest growth?

   Plant A: _____

   Plant B: _____

   Plant C: _____

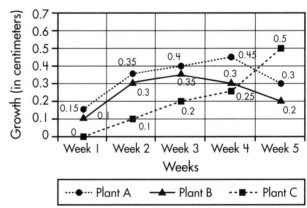

Plant Growth Chart for New Fertilizers

4. Which plant had greater growth each week than the week before from Week 2 to Week 5?

   _____

Lesson 5.6 Circle Graphs

A **circle graph** is used to show parts of a whole. The entire circle represents 100%. The circle is divided into sectors, which are fractional parts of the whole. The table and figure below show how a percentage relates to a fraction and the degree measure of the sectors of a circle.

Sector	Percent	Fraction	Degree Measure
	100%	one whole	360°
A	50%	$\frac{1}{2}$	180°
B	25%	$\frac{1}{4}$	90°
C	12.5%	$\frac{1}{8}$	45°
D	6.25%	$\frac{1}{16}$	22.5°

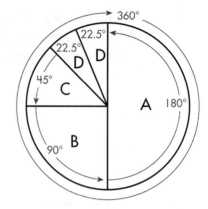

A circle graph can be divided into any number of sectors of any percentage/fraction value. The total will always be 100%, one whole, or 360°. For the circle above,

$180° + 90° + 45° + 22.5° + 22.5° = 360°$, or: $\frac{1}{2} + \frac{1}{4} + \frac{1}{8} + \frac{1}{16} + \frac{1}{16} = 1$

Determine the percentage and number of degrees for each segment. Use a protractor, if necessary.

1. Sector A _____ % or _____°

2. Sector B _____ % or _____°

3. Sector C _____ % or _____°

4. Sector D _____ % or _____°

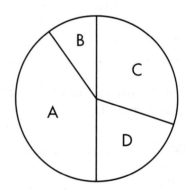

Draw the sectors in the table on the circle to the right. Use a protractor. Label each sector of the circle with the percentage and degree angle.

5.

Sectors
15%
25%
35%
15%
10%

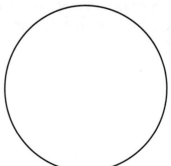

Lesson 5.6 Circle Graphs

A circle graph shows the relationship of each sector to the whole, or 100%.

What are Crawford County's total expenditures for the current year?

$13,573,452

Which category is the greatest portion of the Crawford County yearly expenses?

education

How much did Crawford County spend on insurance in the current year?

$1,044,984, or 8%

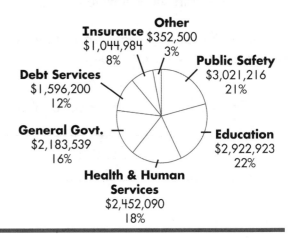

Crawford County Expenditures
Current Year
Total: $13,573,452

Refer to the circle graph and table to answer the following questions.

1. The circle graph and table at right are complete except for the percentages. Calculate the percentage for each income source and write it in the percent column in the table. Round percents to the nearest tenth.

2. What is Crawford County's greatest single

   source of income? _____

3. What total percentage of its income does Crawford County get from grants from the

   state and federal governments? _____

4. Compare the Crawford County Income graph to the graph at the top of this page. Did Crawford County have more income than expenses or more expenses than income? Record the difference.

   _____

   _____

Crawford County Income
Current Year
Total: $14,757,967

Income Source	Percent
Property Tax	
Interest from Reserve Fund	
Sales Tax	
Permits and Fees	
Fines	
State Grants	
Federal Grants	

Check What You Learned

Displaying Data

Use the two data sets below to answer the questions.

Juanita gathered information about the sizes of oranges and grapefruits. She chose 10 of each from the grocery store to weigh.

a   b

1. Draw a histogram for each set of data.

Weight of oranges (oz.)	Weight of grapefruits (oz.)
7.0, 7.5, 7.2, 6.5, 7.8, 7.3, 7.4, 7.7, 7.5, 7.2	10.2, 8.9, 9.4, 9.5, 10.0, 8.9, 9.2, 9.6, 10.1, 9.6

Create a multiple line graph on a separate piece of paper using the information in the table below. When you are finished, refer to the graph to answer the questions.

2. Which age group had the most subscriptions in 2007? _____

   the fewest subscriptions? _____

3. In which year was there a decline in subscriptions in all four age groups?

   _____

4. Which two age groups show the greatest overall potential for growth in subscriptions

   in future years? _____ _____

Mountain Hiking Online Magazine Subscriptions 2007–2010				
Age Group	2007	2008	2009	2010
20–35	8,700	6,320	6,895	7,119
35–50	7,223	7,000	8,778	9,654
50–65	4,002	3,822	6,200	6,620
65–80	1,041	890	1118	1,297

Check What You Know

Scatter Plots and Bivariate Data

Answer the questions by interpreting data from the graph.

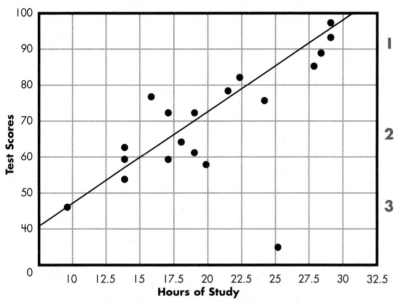

1. What two sets of data are being compared by this scatter plot?

   _____

2. Is the correlation positive or negative?

   _____

3. What is a possible explanation for the outliers?

   _____

Use the data set below to create a scatter plot with a line of best fit. Then, answer the questions.

4.

Dog Sizes	
Height (cm)	Mass (kg)
41	4.5
40	5
35	4
38	3.5
43	5.5
44	5
37	5
39	4
42	4
44	6
31	3.5

5. What two sets of data are being compared by this scatter plot? _____

6. Is the correlation between the data sets positive or negative? _____

7. What is a possible explanation for the outliers? _____

8. If a dog has a mass of 3 kg, predict the height of the dog. _____

Lesson 6.1 Scatter Plots

The data points in a scatter plot are plotted on a coordinate system as ordered pairs.

A **scatter plot** shows the relationship, or correlation, between two sets of data, or variables. The scatter plot to the right shows a positive correlation between weekly practice minutes on the *x*-axis and runs scored on the *y*-axis.

See the line drawn through the data points in the graph on the right. This **line of best fit** can help show the relationship between the two variables in the graph. The line of best fit is drawn so there are about an equal number of data points above and below the line.

What trend in the data is shown by the line of best fit? *As weekly practice minutes increase, the number of runs scored increases.*

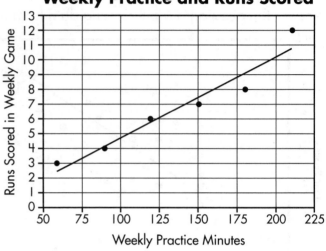

Lorimer High Softball Team Weekly Practice and Runs Scored

Weekly Practice Minutes	60	90	120	150	180	210
Runs Scored	3	4	6	7	8	12

Answer the questions by referring to the scatter plot.

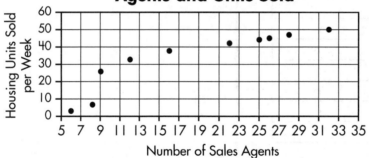

Barker Real Estate Sales Agents and Units Sold

1. What two sets of data are being compared in the scatter plot?

_____

2. Draw a line of best fit on the graph. What general trend does the graph show?

_____

_____

Lesson 6.1 Scatter Plots

When a line of best fit is drawn from the lower left to the upper right, there is a **positive correlation**. This means as x increases, y increases. The x and y variables have a stronger relationship the closer the data points are to the line. Data points in a perfectly straight line show the strongest relationship. A line of best fit may also help identify **outliers**, which are data points that do not conform to the general trend.

A line of best fit may run from the upper left to lower right (see figure at left below). In that case, the correlation is **negative**. Also, sometimes there is no correlation, as shown in the figure below on the right.

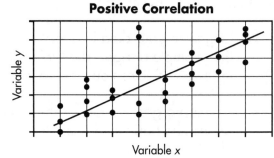

Positive Correlation

As variable x increases, y increases.

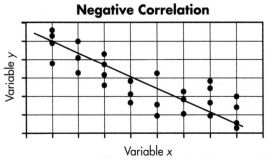

Negative Correlation

As variable x increases, y decreases.

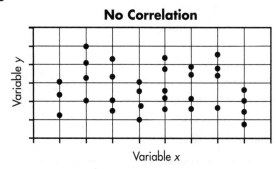

No Correlation

There is no apparent pattern.

Refer to the scatter plot below to answer the questions.

1. Explain the data point located at $98.

   _____

2. What type of correlation is shown by the graph data?

   _____

3. Predict the most likely result of lowering the prices of the pictures priced over $100.

   _____

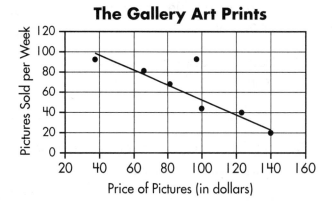

The Gallery Art Prints

Lesson 6.2 Create a Scatter Plot

Follow the steps below to create a scatter plot.

1. Organize your data in a table as shown in the example at right. The table will include the two variables you want to compare.

2. Develop a graph scale for the values on the x-axis (the horizontal axis) and the y-axis (the vertical axis).

3. Provide an overall graph title and a title for each axis.

4. Plot the data on the graph by drawing a dot for each value.

5. When analyzing the data, you may find it helpful to draw a line of best fit, as shown in the graph at right.

Tim Kiley Weekly Earnings

Hours Worked	18	22	25	28	30	32
Weekly Earnings	315	385	437.5	490	525	560

Follow the instructions below to create a scatter plot. Then, answer the questions.

1. On a separate piece of paper, create a scatter plot from the data in the table. Draw a line of best fit.

Age	20	30	40	50	60	70
Minutes of Daily Exercise	110	108	72	64	44	20

2. Does the scatter plot show a correlation? If so, describe it.

_____

3. Predict the number of minutes that an 80-year-old would exercise daily. _____

On a separate piece of paper, create a scatter plot from the data in the table.

4. Does the scatter plot show a correlation? If so, describe it.

_____

_____

Carter High School Basketball Team								
Height (inches)	70	71	72	73	74	75	76	77	78
Average Points per Game	12	14	12	22	12	10	16	18	10

Lesson 6.3 Interpreting Scatter Plots

A **scatter plot** shows the relationship between two sets of data. It is made up of points. The points are plotted by using the values from the two sets of data as coordinates.

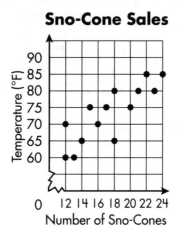

Sno-Cone Sales

This scatter plot shows the relationship between the temperature and the number of sno-cones sold. As one value increases, the other appears to increase as well. This indicates a *positive* relationship.

A *negative* relationship would show that more sno-cones are sold as the temperature decreases.

No relationship would show no clear trend in the data.

Use the scatter plot above to complete the data table. Include the coordinates for all 14 points.

1.

Sno-Cones	12	12	13	14										
Temperature	60	70	60	65										

Does each scatter plot below indicate a *positive* relationship, a *negative* relationship, or *no relationship*?

2.

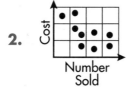

Number Sold

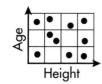

Height

Weight

_____   _____   _____

Use the data below to create a scatter plot on the grid. Be sure to include all labels.

3.

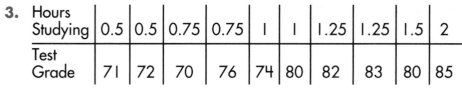

Hours Studying	0.5	0.5	0.75	0.75	1	1	1.25	1.25	1.5	2
Test Grade	71	72	70	76	74	80	82	83	80	85

Lesson 6.3 Interpreting Scatter Plots

A **scatter plot** is a graph that shows the relationship between two sets of data. To see the relationship clearly, a **line of best fit**, or trend line, can be drawn. This is drawn so that there are about the same number of data points above and below the line.

This scatter plot shows the relationship between average high temperature and a family's gas use for heating fuel each month.

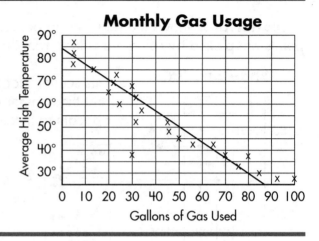

Monthly Gas Usage

Answer the questions by interpreting data from the scatter plots.

Age and Height Poll Results

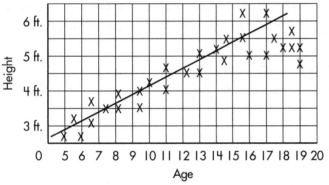

1. Which two sets of data are being compared by this scatter plot?

   _____

2. Is the correlation positive or negative?

   _____

3. How many people were polled? _____

4. How do you explain the data points at the end that do not follow the line of best fit?

   _____

5. Which two pieces of data are being compared by this scatter plot?

   _____

6. Draw the line of best fit. Is the correlation positive or negative? _____

7. There are a few outliers for this scatter plot. What do they show? _____

8. What is a possible explanation? _____

   _____

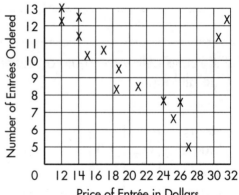

Ordering Trends at Chez Henri

Lesson 6.4 Fitting Lines to Scatter Plots

When **bivariate data**, data with two variables, is graphed on a scatter plot, it may have a positive or negative association. A trend line can be used to make predictions about values that are not included in the data set. The accuracy of the prediction will depend on how closely the trend line fits the data points.

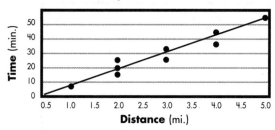

Create a trend line by using a straight edge to draw a line across the points on a scatter plot. Attempt to have the same number of points above and below the trend line while ignoring outliers.

Based on this trend line, at a distance of 3.5 miles, the time should be about 37 minutes.

Create a trend line for each scatter plot shown below.

a

b

1.

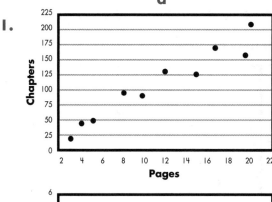

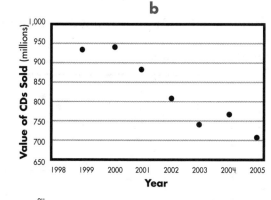

2.

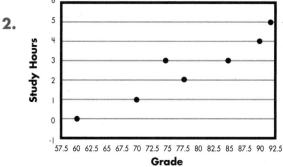

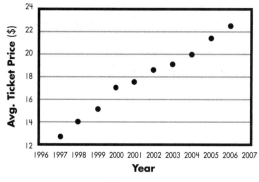

3.

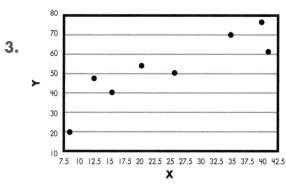

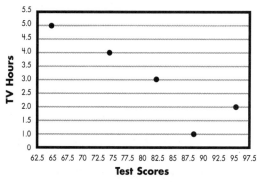

Lesson 6.4 Fitting Lines to Scatter Plots

Create a trend line for each scatter plot shown below. Then, make a prediction about the value of one variable given one value of the other variable.

a

b

1.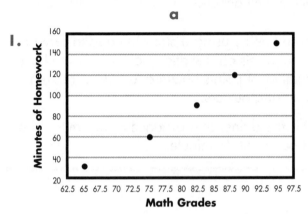

If a student does 80 minutes of homework,

predict his grade. _____

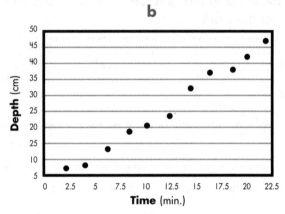

If the water is measured at 13 minutes,

predict its depth. _____

2.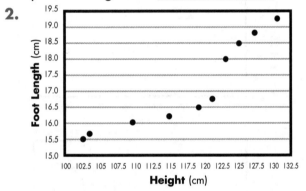

If someone is 106 cm tall, predict

his/her foot length. _____

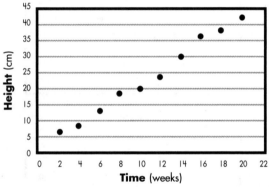

If the plant is measured at 15 weeks,

predict its height. _____

3.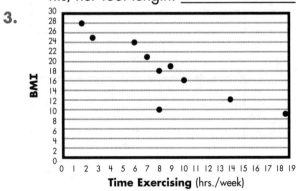

If a person spends 17 hours a week

exercising, predict her BMI. _____

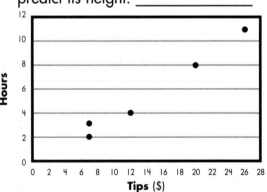

If a server spends 12 hours a week working,

predict the tips he will earn. _____

Lesson 6.5 Creating Equations to Solve Bivariate Problems

When given a set of bivariate data with a fairly consistent rate of change, a scatter plot with a trend line can be used to create an equation that will approximate the relationship between the two sets of data.

Temp. (°F)	Ice Cream Sales ($)
57.6	215
61.5	325
53.4	185
59.4	332
65.3	406
71.8	522
66.9	412

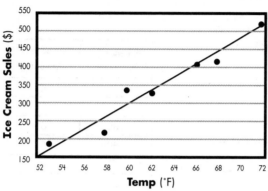

Step 1: Use the data set to create a scatter plot with a trend line.

Step 2: Use the 2 points of data closest to the trend line to find the slope of the trend line.

Step 3: Use one point of data with the calculated slope to find the y-intersect of the trend line.

Step 4: Use the calculated slope and y-intersect to state the equation in linear form, $y = mx + b$.

$$m = \frac{522 - 406}{71.8 - 65.3} = \frac{116}{6.5} = 17.85 \qquad 406 = (17.85)(65.3) + b$$

$$y = 17.85x - 759.61 \qquad\qquad b = -759.61$$

Use each set of bivariate data to create a scatter plot, trend line, and an equation that approximates the data set.

1.

a

x	y
2	5
4	15
5	25
1	2
7	20
4	8
6	10
1	1
3	12

equation:

_____

b

Hours	Wages ($)
8	300
6	200
10	500
9	400
4	100
12	700
14	1000
5	150
2	50

equation:

_____

Lesson 6.5 Creating Equations to Solve Bivariate Problems

Use each set of bivariate data to create a scatter plot, trend line, and an equation that approximates the data set. What does the slope mean? What does the *y*-intercept mean or is the *y*-intercept not meaningful in this context?

a

1.

Hours	Test Score
18	59
16	67
22	74
27	90
15	62
28	89
18	71
19	60
22	84
30	98

equation:

_____

slope:

_____

_____

y-intercept:

_____

_____

b

Population (hundred thousands)	Number of Schools
110	4
130	4
130	6
140	5
150	6
160	8
170	7
180	8
190	9

equation:

_____

slope:

_____

_____

y-intercept:

_____

_____

2.

Temp. (°F)	Ice Cream Sales ($)
57	125
60	175
53	100
59	130
65	275
71	405
66	295
77	735
73	525
62	200

equation:

_____

slope:

_____

_____

y-intercept:

_____

_____

Amount of Time in the Sun (hours)	Sunflower Height (cm)
2	15
4	19
6	25
3	17
5	22
7	30
2	14
4	20
5	23
6	24

equation:

_____

slope:

_____

_____

y-intercept:

_____

_____

Lesson 6.5 Creating Equations to Solve Bivariate Problems

Use each set of bivariate data to create a scatter plot, trend line, and an equation that approximates the data set. What does the slope mean? What does the *y*-intercept mean or is the *y*-intercept not meaningful in this context?

a

1.

Time (hours)	Cost of Job ($)
5	1000
7	1000
5	1500
8	1200
10	2000
13	2500
15	2800
20	3200
25	4000

equation:

_____

slope:

_____

_____

y-intercept:

_____

_____

b

Time (hours)	Score
4	15
5	16
5	20
10	12
15	8
10	8
20	5
15	4
15	12

equation:

_____

slope:

_____

_____

y-intercept:

_____

_____

2.

Time (hours)	Money ($)
2	15
4	20
6	23
7	24
3	17
10	50
9	42
4	22
5	24
7	26

equation:

_____

slope:

_____

_____

y-intercept:

_____

_____

Height (inches)	Distance (miles)
62	9.3
64	9.7
67	10.2
71	11.5
75	13.5
78	15.6
63	9.4
55	8.6
53	8.2
51	7.9

equation:

_____

slope:

_____

_____

y-intercept:

_____

_____

Lesson 6.6 Problem Solving

Solve each problem.

1. Wally's Sport Shop has its best sales in the summer months selling fishing equipment. In the table below, Wally recorded his summer sales data. For an overview, he would like to see it in a bar chart format. Create a bar chart on the blank graph below. Make sure to provide a scale for the frequency axis, category labels, axis labels, and a graph title. Also, draw in the bars.

	Sales Dollars (thousands)
April	26
May	45
June	65
July	72
Aug.	68
Sept.	55

2. Refer to the graph you created in problem 1. In which month did sales peak and begin to decline? _____

3. The East Side Softball League is made up of teams from four local communities that play teams in other towns. Answer the following questions about the graph below.

a. Which team had the poorest record from 2006 to 2010?

_____

b. Which team had the most wins in all but one season?

_____

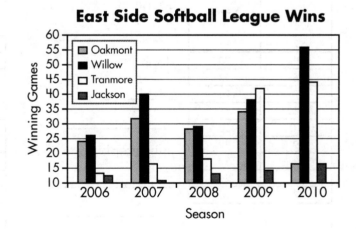

c. Which team had more wins each year than the year before from 2007 to 2010?

_____

d. How many more wins did Oakmont have in 2009 than in 2010? _____

Lesson 6.6 Problem Solving

Solve each problem.

4. Mr. Alvarez wants to reduce his family's expenses. He put the family's expense data in the circle graph at right. Mr. Alvarez thinks that three categories of expenses could be reduced: cell phones, cars, and entertainment.

   a. How much does the family spend altogether on cell phones, cars, and entertainment each month?

   _____

   b. Cell phones, cars, and entertainment add up to what percentage of the family's monthly expenses?

   _____

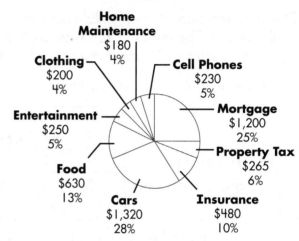

5. Mr. Alvarez put his family on a budget. He tracked their total income and expenses for the next six months, as shown in the graph.

   a. In which months did the family spend less than the average monthly expenses shown in the circle graph at the top of this page?

   _____

   b. In which months did expenses almost equal income?

   _____

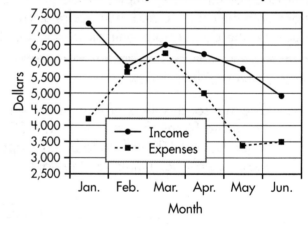

6. Pat's 2-pound trout stopped gaining weight, so she fed them a new fish food. She tracked their weights for five weeks. The data is in the scatter plot at the right. Draw a line of best fit. Then, predict the approximate weight of most of the fish if Pat feeds them the special food for a sixth week.

   _____

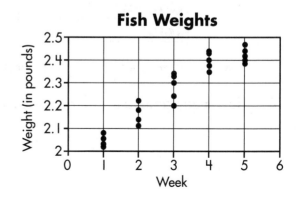

Lesson 6.7 Two-Way Tables

A **two-way table** summarizes data from two categorical variables collected from the same subjects by showing the frequency, or count, of the data.

A two-way table is created for the following data.

One hundred students with cellphones are surveyed on storing their picture and their home address on the phone. The results were 70 students store their picture, 50 students store their address, and 30 students store both their picture and their address.

The two-way table below shows the results. The given results are written in shaded cells.

	Address Stored	**No Address Stored**	**Total**
Picture stored	30	50 – 10 = 40	70
No picture stored	50 – 30 = 20	30 – 20 = 10	100 – 70 = 30
Total	50	100 – 50 = 50	100

The rows represent the category picture stored and the columns represent the category address stored. There are total cells for both the row frequencies and column frequencies. The last cell of the last column gives the total frequency. The interior cells give the frequency of the intersection of a row and column. For example, the 30 in row 2, column 2 represents the frequency of students who store both their picture and their address. The 20 in row 3, column 2 represents the frequency of students who do not store their picture but do store their address.

Answer the problems below.

1. One thousand college graduates are surveyed to determine where they will travel outside of the United States. It was found that 450 graduates will go to Europe, 310 will go to South America, and 120 will go to both Europe and South America. Complete the two-way table, shown below, to summarize the data.

	Europe	**Not Europe**	**Total**
South America			
Not South America			
Total			

2. How many graduates will go to Europe and not South America? _____

3. How many graduates will go to neither Europe nor South America? _____

Lesson 6.7 Two-Way Tables

A two-way table can show relative frequencies. **Relative frequency** is the ratio of the frequency of a subtotal in a category to the frequency of the total in the category. A relative frequency table shows ratios to compare the data. Relative frequency can be calculated for the whole table, the row categories, or the column categories. To calculate relative frequencies, divide the frequency of the subtotal by the frequency of the total. The relative frequencies are experimental probabilities.

One hundred sixty freshmen and sophomores are asked how they get their news. The results are in the frequency table shown below.

	TV	Internet	Total
Freshman	50	12	62
Sophomore	20	78	98
Total	70	90	160

To create a relative frequency table for the whole table, divide each cell by the total frequency 160.

	TV	Internet	Total
Freshman	$\frac{50}{160} = 0.3125$	$\frac{12}{160} = 0.075$	$\frac{62}{160} = 0.3875$
Sophomore	$\frac{20}{160} = 0.125$	$\frac{78}{160} = 0.4875$	$\frac{98}{160} = 0.6125$
Total	$\frac{70}{160} = 0.4375$	$\frac{90}{160} = 0.5625$	$\frac{160}{160} = 1$

Answer the problems below.

1. One-hundred high school seniors are surveyed to determine whether they studied Spanish or French. It was found that 31 studied French, 45 studied Spanish, and 12 studied both Spanish and French. Complete a two-way relative frequency table for the whole table shown below.

	Spanish	Not Spanish	Total
French			
Not French			
Total			

2. What is the probability that a student studied French but not Spanish?

_____

3. What is the probability that a student studied both Spanish and French?

_____

Check What You Learned

Scatter Plots and Bivariate Data

Use each set of bivariate data to create a scatter plot, trend line, and an equation that approximates the data set.

a

1.

Time Testing (min.)	Test Grade
31	64
38	66
46	82
49	90
20	52
35	66
40	79
52	95

equation:

_____

b

Hours Worked	Paycheck ($)
12	54
13	56
16	65
17	64
20	100
10	50
12	55
18	70

equation:

_____

Students were asked if they swim and run. The survey showed that out of 250 students, 100 swim, 160 run, and 25 do neither.

2. Create a two-way table to represent the data from the survey.

3. How many students swim and do not run? _____

4. How many students run and do not swim? _____

5. How many students swim and run? _____

Final Test Chapters 1–6

Solve the problems based on one spin of the spinner. Express each probability as a fraction in simplest form.

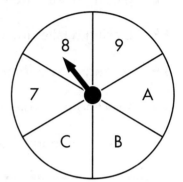

1. The number of possible outcomes is _____.

2. The probability of stopping on 8 is _____.

3. The probability of stopping on a letter is _____.

4. The probability of stopping on a number is _____.

5. The probability of stopping on a vowel is _____.

Solve the problem. Express probability as a fraction in simplest form.

6. Events Y and Z are mutually exclusive. $P(Y) = \frac{5}{8}$. $P(Z)$ is $\frac{1}{16}$. What is the probability that either Y or Z will occur?

    P(Y) or P(Z) is _____

Solve each problem. Express probabilities as fractions in simplest form.

7. Events C and D are independent. The probability that C will occur is $\frac{1}{3}$. The probability that D will occur is $\frac{1}{4}$. What is the probability that both C and D will occur?

    The probability that both C and D will occur is _____

8. A bag contains 10 white toys and 12 green toys. What is the probability of choosing a white toy and then a green toy? (After choosing it, you would not replace the white toy.)

    The probability of choosing a white toy and then a green toy is _____

Find the mean, median, mode, and range of each set of data. Round to the nearest tenth.

		a	b	c	d
		mean:	median:	mode:	range:
9.	8, 12, 8, 7, 11	mean: _____	median: _____	mode: _____	range: _____
10.	32, 15, 18, 14, 30, 27	mean: _____	median: _____	mode: _____	range: _____
11.	5, 7, 2, 13, 11, 17, 14, 13	mean: _____	median: _____	mode: _____	range: _____

Final Test Chapters 1–6

Write *yes* or *no* to tell if each situation describes uniform probability.

12. picking a letter from the word "uniform" _____

13. picking a letter from the word "probability" _____

14. picking a card from a deck of 26 cards _____

15. selecting a marble from a sack of 4 blue marbles and 3 red marbles _____

16. picking an apple from a bin of 25 organic and 20 non-organic apples _____

Answer the problems below. Express each probability as a fraction in simplest terms.

The spinner at the right is spun 30 times. Out of the 30 times, it lands 5 times on 1, 12 times on 2, 10 times on 3, and 3 times on 4.

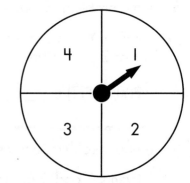

17. What is the experimental probability of landing on 3?

_____

18. What is the theoretical probability of landing on 3?

_____

19. What is the experimental probability of landing on an odd number? _____

20. What is the theoretical probability of landing on an odd number? _____

Determine the probability. Express the answer as a fraction in simplest form.

21. Events A and B are independent. The probability that A will occur is $\frac{5}{8}$. The probability that B

will occur is $\frac{1}{3}$. What is the probability that both A and B will occur? _____

Final Test Chapters 1–6

Solve the problems below. Express each probability as a fraction in simplest terms.

22. A jar of marbles has 8 yellow, 3 red, and 9 green marbles. You select 1 marble, put it back, and then select another. What is the probability that you choose 2 red marbles? _____

23. Two cards are drawn from a deck of cards numbered 1 through 20, inclusive. If a card is drawn and not replaced, what is the probability of drawing a card that is not numbered 5?

_____

24. A fruit bowl has 5 apples and 3 oranges in it. What is the probability of choosing an apple and then an orange if the fruit you choose is not replaced? _____

Solve the problems below. Express each probability as a fraction in simplest terms.

A blanket is sold in two sizes, small and large, and three colors, red, blue, and beige.

25. Create a tree diagram to display the situation above.

26. What is the probability someone buys a small blanket? _____

27. What is the probability someone buys a red blanket? _____

28. What is the probability someone buys a small red blanket? _____

Use the line plot to answer the questions.

29. What is the mode? _____

30. What is the range? _____

31. What is the median? _____

32. How many months does the plot include? _____

**Car Accidents per Month
for a Period of 2 Years in Websterville**

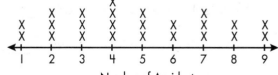

Number of Accidents

Final Test Chapters 1–6

Refer to the circle graph to answer the questions.

33. What does the graph show?

_____

34. What is Jan's greatest source of income?

_____

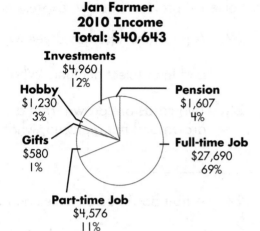

Jan Farmer
2010 Income
Total: $40,643

Investments
$4,960
12%

Hobby
$1,230
3%

Pension
$1,607
4%

Gifts
$580
1%

Full-time Job
$27,690
69%

Part-time Job
$4,576
11%

Refer to the line graph to answer the questions.

35. What does the graph show? _____

_____

36. In which year did expenses equal income?

_____

37. In which year were savings greater than expenses?

_____

38. In which years did expenses decline from the previous year?

_____

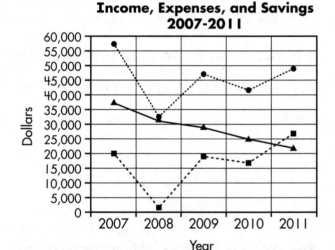

Jan Farmer
Income, Expenses, and Savings
2007-2011

···•··· Income   —▲— Expenses   --■-- Savings

Read each question and write *statistical* or *not statistical*.

39. How many students passed? _____

40. What is the average fee paid? _____

41. How much do these sandals cost? _____

42. Who is the tallest in the class? _____

Final Test   Chapters 1–6

Tell if each sample would be considered *random* or *biased*.

43. Surveying women in a yoga class about the benefits of taking yoga. _____

44. Asking a class of law students to give opinions about the state of the legal industry.

_____

45. Every 10th student that enters a school cafeteria is asked to reveal their favorite beverage for

lunch _____

Biologists were concerned about the declining population of a rare lizard, so they restricted human access to the lizard breeding area. The biologists then collected population data for 6 years. Refer to the scatter plot to answer the questions.

46. In which year did limiting human access to the area begin to affect the lizard population?

_____

47. The outlier appears at (circle the correct answer):   (0, 400)   (6, 650)   (5, 300)

48. Does the scatter plot show a positive correlation, a negative correlation, or no correlation?

_____

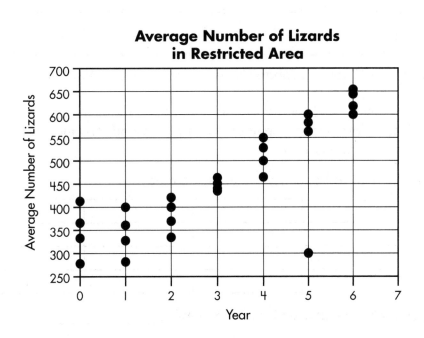

Average Number of Lizards in Restricted Area

Final Test Chapters 1–6

Solve the problems below. Express probability as a fraction in simplest terms.

49. Darleen uses a random number generator on the Internet to simulate rolling a die 60 times. She generates 60 random numbers from 1 to 6 inclusive to represent the numbers on a die. The numbers Darleen generates are shown below.

1	1	5	6	2	6	3	5	6	2
6	1	3	1	5	1	1	4	2	4
1	4	4	2	2	2	1	1	1	2
3	6	5	3	4	4	6	5	3	1
4	5	2	2	6	3	3	4	6	4
3	3	2	5	2	2	5	1	2	5

Based on the results of the simulation, what is the probability of rolling an even number?

_____

50. A charity contacted 70 people by phone and 150 people by email. Donations were made by 20% of the people contacted by email. Donations were not made by 38 people who were contacted by phone. Make a two-way table with the categories *method of contact* and *donations*.

Solve the problems below. Express probability as a fraction in simplest terms.

At a high school, 400 juniors and seniors are surveyed to see whether they are in a club or not. There is a total of 220 juniors and seniors that are in a club and 210 juniors that are surveyed. The number of juniors in a club is 150.

51. Make a two-way relative frequency table for the data.

52. What is the probability that a senior is in a club? _____

Scoring Record for Posttests, Mid-Test, and Final Test

Chapter Posttest	Your Score	Performance			
		Excellent	Very Good	Fair	Needs Improvement
1	____ of 10	10	9	8	7 or fewer
2	____ of 16	15–16	13–14	11–12	10 or fewer
3	____ of 11	11	10	9	8 or fewer
4	____ of 33	30–33	27–29	24–26	23 or fewer
5	____ of 5	5	4	3	2 or fewer
6	____ of 6	6	5	4	3 or fewer
Mid-Test	____ of 51	46–51	14–45	40–36	35 or fewer
Final Test	____ of 61	55–61	49–54	43–48	42 or fewer

Record your test score in the Your Score column. See where your score falls in the Performance columns. Your score is based on the total number of required responses. If your score is fair or needs improvement, review the chapter material.

Data Analysis and Probability Answers

Chapter 1

Check What You Know, page 1

1. $\frac{1}{8}$
2. $\frac{1}{2}$
3. $\frac{1}{2}$
4. $\frac{1}{3}$
5a. penny
5b. $\frac{3}{5}$
6. no
7. no
8. yes
9. $\frac{7}{13}$
10a. $\frac{51}{100}$
10b. experimental

Lesson 1.1, page 2

	a	b
1.	heads, tails	yes
2.	2, 3, 4, 5, 6, 7, 8, 9, 10, 11, 12	Answers will vary.
3.	red marble, green marble	red marble
4.	all names	yes

Lesson 1.1, page 3

1. $\frac{1}{2}$
2. $\frac{1}{3}$
3. $\frac{1}{6}$
4. $\frac{1}{3}$
5. $\frac{1}{6}$
6. $\frac{1}{6}$
7. $\frac{1}{3}$
8. 0

Lesson 1.1, page 4

1. 5
2. $\frac{1}{5}$
3. $\frac{3}{5}$
4. $\frac{2}{5}$
5. $\frac{2}{5}$
6. $\frac{4}{5}$
7. $\frac{2}{9}$
8. $\frac{7}{9}$
9. $\frac{2}{3}$
10. 0

Lesson 1.1, page 5

11. $\frac{3}{7}$
12. $\frac{1}{7}$
13. $\frac{8}{15}$
14. $\frac{7}{15}$
15. 8
16. $\frac{1}{8}$
17. $\frac{1}{4}$

Lesson 1.2, page 6

1. $\frac{2}{3}$
2. $\frac{5}{8}$
3. $\frac{1}{2}$
4. $\frac{3}{8}$

Lesson 1.2, page 7

1. $\frac{3}{10}$
2. $\frac{2}{5}$
3. $\frac{1}{5}$
4. $\frac{1}{10}$
5. $\frac{1}{2}$
6. $\frac{1}{3}$
7. $\frac{1}{6}$
8. $\frac{1}{6}$
9. $\frac{1}{6}$
10. $\frac{1}{3}$

Lesson 1.2, page 8

1. $\frac{1}{2}$
2. $\frac{3}{10}$
3. $\frac{1}{5}$
4. $\frac{7}{10}$
5. $\frac{1}{3}$
6. $\frac{1}{6}$
7. $\frac{1}{6}$
8. $\frac{5}{12}$
9. $\frac{1}{3}$
10. $\frac{1}{3}$
11. $\frac{1}{3}$
12. $\frac{1}{6}$
13. $\frac{5}{12}$
14. $\frac{1}{3}$
15. $\frac{1}{4}$

Lesson 1.3, page 9

	a	b
1.	yes	no
2.	yes	no
3.	no	yes
4.	no	no
5.	no	no
6.	no	yes

Data Analysis and Probability Answers

Lesson 1.3, page 10
Answers will vary.
1. Spinner must have an equal number of same size spaces with an equal number of stars and diamonds.
2. Spinner must have an equal number of same size spaces with numbers 1, 2, 3, and 4.
3. ⬤⬤⬤⬤⬤⬤⬤⬤
4. Answers will vary but may include

Lesson 1.4, page 11

	a	b
1.	not equal	equal
2.	equal	not equal
3.	equal	equal
4.	not equal	not equal

Lesson 1.4, page 12
1.

2.

3.

Lesson 1.4, page 13
1a. $\frac{2}{6}$ or $\frac{1}{3}$ 1b. $\frac{3}{6}$ or $\frac{1}{2}$

2a. $\frac{1}{2}$ 2b. $\frac{1}{2}$

3a. $\frac{11}{90}$ 3b. $\frac{10}{85}$ or $\frac{2}{17}$

3c. the first bag

4a. $\frac{16}{25}$ 4b. $\frac{12}{19}$

Lesson 1.5, page 14
1. $\frac{1}{6}$
2. 30
3. $\frac{2}{5}$
4. $\frac{1}{6}$
5. $\frac{2}{5}$
6. $\frac{1}{4}$

Lesson 1.5, page 15
7a. $\frac{1}{12}$ 7b. $\frac{1}{6}$

7c. theoretical, $\frac{1}{12}$ 7d. $\frac{5}{9}$

7e. $\frac{1}{2}$ 7f. experimental, $\frac{1}{18}$

8a. $\frac{1}{6}$ 8b. $\frac{1}{6}$

8c. They are the same.   8d. $\frac{71}{144}$

8e. $\frac{1}{2}$ 8f. theoretical, $\frac{1}{144}$

Lesson 1.6, page 16
1. 0.42
2. 0.45; yes
3. 0.81

Lesson 1.6, page 17
4. Generate random integers from 1 to 4, inclusive. Let 1 be a success. 2, 3, or 4 is a failure.
5. Generate random integers from 1 to 6, inclusive. Let 2, 4, or 6 be a success. 1, 3, or 5 is a failure.

Check What You Learned, page 18
1. $\frac{1}{2}$
2. $\frac{3}{8}$
3. $\frac{5}{26}$
4a. $\frac{2}{5}$
4b. $\frac{1}{5}$
5. $\frac{2}{5}$
6. yes
7. yes
8. no
9. $\frac{79}{100}$

Data Analysis and Probability Answers

Chapter 2

Check What You Know, page 19

1.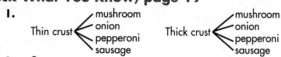

2. 8
3. $\frac{1}{8}$
4. $\frac{2}{9}$
5. $\frac{1}{720}$
6. $\frac{1}{4}$
7. $\frac{1}{6}$
8. $\frac{1}{26}$
9. $\frac{1}{16}$
10. $\frac{1}{3}$

Lesson 2.1, page 20

1. 12

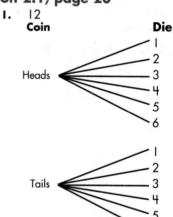

Lesson 2.1, page 21

1.

		small
red		medium
		large
blue		small / medium / large
tie-dyed		small / medium / large

1a. 9   1b. $\frac{1}{3}$

2a. 8   2b. $\frac{1}{2}$ 2c. $\frac{1}{4}$ 2d. $\frac{1}{8}$

Lesson 2.2, page 22

1. $\frac{6}{35}$
2. $\frac{9}{25}$
3. $\frac{1}{4}$
4. $\frac{9}{64}$

Lesson 2.2, page 23

1. $\frac{1}{8}$
2. $\frac{9}{10}$
3. $\frac{1}{10}$
4. $\frac{1}{220}$

Lesson 2.2, page 24

	a	b
1.	36	12
2.	8	104
3.	36	72
4.	208	144

Lesson 2.3, page 25

1. 288
2. 60
3. 320
4. 20
5. 180
6. 192
7. 280

Lesson 2.4, page 26

1. 12

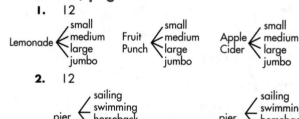

2. 12

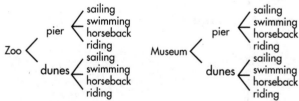

Lesson 2.4, page 27

1. 8
2. 18
3. 6; J ⟨ K—L / L—K   K ⟨ J—L / L—J   L ⟨ K—J / J—K

Data Analysis and Probability Answers

Lesson 2.4, page 28

1.

	black	brown	blue	khaki
black	bl/bl	bl/br	bl/blu	bl/k
blue	blu/bl	blu/br	blu/blu	blu/k
red	r/bl	r/bl	r/bl	r/k
green	g/bl	g/br	g/blu	g/k
yellow	y/bl	y/br	y/blu	y/k

$\frac{2}{20}$ or $\frac{1}{10}$

2.

	1	2	3	4	5	6	7	8
1	2	3	4	5	6	7	8	9
2	3	4	5	6	7	8	9	10
3	4	5	6	7	8	9	10	11
4	5	6	7	8	9	10	11	12
5	6	7	8	9	10	11	12	13
6	7	8	9	10	11	12	13	14

$\frac{5}{48}$

Lesson 2.5, page 29

Strategies will vary.
1. 8
2. 20
3. $\frac{1}{9}$
4. $\frac{1}{26}$

Lesson 2.5, page 30

Strategies will vary.
1. $\frac{1}{25}$
2. 48
3. 27
4. $\frac{1}{8}$

Lesson 2.5, page 31

Strategies will vary.
1. 36
2. $\frac{1}{6}$
3. $\frac{1}{9}$
4. 12

Lesson 2.5, page 32

1. $\frac{1}{6}$
2. $\frac{1}{3}$
3. $\frac{5}{6}$
4. $\frac{1}{36}$
5. $\frac{1}{5}$
6. $\frac{7}{10}$
7. $\frac{2}{15}$
8. $\frac{13}{15}$

Lesson 2.5, page 33

1.

CHART

Spinner	Coin	
	Heads	**Tails**
1	H1	T1
2	H2	T2
3	H3	T3
4	H4	T4

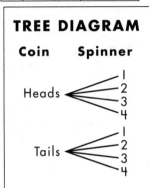

TREE DIAGRAM

Coin   Spinner

Heads — 1, 2, 3, 4

Tails — 1, 2, 3, 4

2. 8
3. 12.5%
4. 87.5%
5. 25.0%

Check What You Learned, page 34

1. $\frac{1}{13}$
2. $\frac{1}{4}$
3. $\frac{17}{52}$
4. $\frac{3}{4}$
5. $\frac{1}{167}$
6. $\frac{1}{16}$
7. $\frac{1}{52}$
8. $\frac{4}{663}$
9. $\frac{13}{204}$

Data Analysis and Probability Answers

Check What You Learned, page 35

10. $\frac{5}{57}$

11. $\frac{20}{171}$

12.

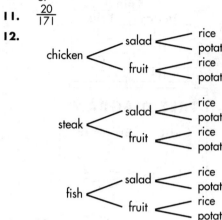

13. 12
14. 50.0%
15. 16.7%
16. 8.3%

Chapter 3

Check What You Know, page 36

1. statistical
2. not statistical
3. statistical
4. not statistical
5. biased
6. random
7. random
8. 30
9. 175
10. $\frac{20}{50}$ or $\frac{2}{5}$

Lesson 3.1, page 37

	a	b
1.	statistical	not
2.	statistical	statistical
3.	not	not
4.	not	statistical
5.	not	statistical

Lesson 3.1, page 38

Answers may vary.

1. How tall are the students in my school?
2. What scores did students score on the last spelling test?
3. How many pages are in the typical 6th grade novel?
4. How many students are there per PE class in my school?
5. How much do average apples cost?
6. What is the most popular car in the U.S.?
7. How many minutes do children exercise per week?

Lesson 3.2, page 40

Step 5. Interpretations will vary, but they should answer the original question, including a comparison between males and females. Example: Dogs are the most popular pet overall, but males prefer dogs more strongly than females do.

Lesson 3.3, page 41

1. random
2. biased
3. biased
4. random
5. random
6. biased

Lesson 3.3, page 42

1. systematic random
2. simple random
3. systematic random
4. stratified random
5. voluntary response

Lesson 3.4, page 43

1. 5
2. 16.67%
3. 20 or 21
4. 26.67%
5. 33 or 34
6. 20

Lesson 3.4, page 44

1. 20%
2. 36
3. 108
4. 9
5. 30%
6. 9

Lesson 3.4, page 45

1. 20
2. 100
3. 25%
4. 25
5. 35
6. 40

Data Analysis and Probability Answers

Check What You Learned, page 46
1. not statistical
2. statistical
3. not statistical
4. statistical

	a	b
5.	biased	random
6.	random	random

7. 22
8. 7
9. $\frac{10}{40}$ or $\frac{1}{4}$

Mid-Test, page 47

1a. $\frac{7}{15}$	1b. $\frac{2}{15}$	1c. $\frac{2}{5}$	1d. $\frac{8}{15}$

2. $\frac{1}{2}$

3a. $\frac{1}{4}$	3b. $\frac{1}{36}$		
4a. $\frac{1}{12}$	4b. $\frac{1}{4}$	4c. $\frac{1}{4}$	
5a. $\frac{7}{10}$	5b. $\frac{3}{10}$	5c. $\frac{7}{30}$	
6a. $\frac{1}{4}$	6b. $\frac{1}{2}$		
7a. $\frac{1}{2}$	7b. $\frac{9}{20}$	7c. $\frac{1}{2}$	

Mid-Test, page 48
8. no
9. yes
10. no
11. no
12. $\frac{199}{200}$
13. 282
14. $\frac{5}{9}$
15a. 12
15b. Possible answer. Use a random number generator. Generate random 0s and 1s; 0 = heads 1 = tails; generate random 1, 2, 3, 4, 5, 6 for the number the die lands on.
15c. $\frac{1}{12}$
16. Tree diagram is below:

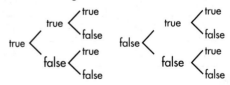

Possible combinations = 8
TTT – TTF – TFT – TFF
FTT – FTF – FFT – FFF

Mid-Test, page 49
17. $\frac{1}{20}$
18. $\frac{1}{216}$
19. $\frac{1}{100}$
20. 15,600

21a. statistical	21f. statistical
21b. statistical	21g. not statistical
21c. not statistical	21h. not statistical
21d. not statistical	21i. statistical
21e. statistical	21j. not statistical

Mid-Test, page 50
22. biased
23. random
24. biased
25. biased
26. random
27. 100
28. 525
29. $\frac{1}{1000}$

Check What You Know, page 51

1.		a	b	c
	mean:	6.4	21	3.5
	median:	8	20.5	3.5
	mode:	9	17	none
	range:	7	15	7

2a. $\frac{80 + 86 + 79 + 81 + n}{5} = 84$
2b. 94
3a. $\frac{720}{n} = 24$
3b. 30
4. 32, 35, 37
5. 61
6. 44
7. 21
8. 40

Data Analysis and Probability Answers

Check What You Know, page 52

9.

Popularity of Colors for Cars			
Color	Frequency	Cumulative Frequency	Relative Frequency
red	25	25	17.9%
blue	20	45	14.3%
black	16	61	11.4%
silver	43	104	30.7%
white	36	140	25.7%

10. 140
11. silver
12. 40%
13. 7
14. 8
15. 20
16. 7.5
17. 12
18. 14
19. 8

Lesson 4.1, page 53

	a	b
1.	mean: 20	mean: $27\frac{1}{2}$
	median: 20	median: $26\frac{1}{2}$
	mode: 25	mode: 21, 36
2.	mean: 17	mean: $18\frac{1}{2}$
	median: 8	median: 5
	mode: none	mode: 0

Lesson 4.1, page 54

1. 81, 84, 88, 93, 97
   mean: 88.6; median: 88; mode: none; range: 16
2. 83, 84, 84, 85, 86
   mean: 84.4; median: 84; mode: 84; range: 3
3. 85, 88, 90, 92, 92
   mean: 89.4; median: 90; mode: 92; range: 7
4. Kara, because her scores had the smallest range

Lesson 4.1, page 55

	a	b
1.	$9.41	$9.75
2.	$9.50	$8.25
3.	$9.50; $10	$8

4. Sam's Pet World pays better. The $20 wage in the set for Beth's Pets is an outlier that increases the mean above Sam's. However, the higher median and mode show that most of Sam's employees are paid better.
5. the mean, because it provides the highest value for this set of wages

Lesson 4.1, page 56

1. 17
2. 34
3. $285

Lesson 4.2, page 57

	a	b
1.	3	5
2.	10	10
3.	8	4
4.	11	14
5.	7	9

Lesson 4.3, page 58

	a	b
1.	5; 2; 7; 5	85; 75; 92.5; 17.5
2.	90; 72.5; 97.5; 25	12; 5; 43; 38
3.	16.5; 4; 39; 35	29; 16; 64; 48

Lesson 4.4, page 59

1a. 15.29; 5.29, 5.29,0.29,0.29, 0.71, 2.71, 7.71; 3.18
1b. 48.29; 10.29, 7.29, 3.29, 2.71, 3.71, 6.71, 7.71; 5.96
2a. 17.57; 7.57, 6.57, 5.57, 0.43, 4.43, 7.43, 7.43; 5.63
2b. 45.1; 34.1, 23.1, 23.1, 12.1, 1.1, 9.9, 9.9, 9.9, 20.9, 42.9; 18.7

Lesson 4.5, page 60

1. 37; 16.5; 9
2. 35; 14; 8
3. 76; 37; 19.1
4. 8; 4; 2.04
5. 62; 16; 13.08
6. 42; 23; 12

Lesson 4.6, page 61

Pet Ownership				
Number of Pets	Frequency	Cumulative Frequency	Relative Frequency (fraction)	Relative Frequency (percent)
0	8	8	$\frac{2}{15}$	13.3%
1	29	37	$\frac{29}{60}$	48.3%
2	15	52	$\frac{1}{4}$	25.0%
3	6	58	$\frac{1}{10}$	10%
4+	2	60	$\frac{1}{30}$	3.3%

1. 60
2. $\frac{7}{20}$

Data Analysis and Probability Answers

Lesson 4.6, page 62

Points Scored per Basketball Game			
Points	Frequency	Cumulative Frequency	Relative Frequency
30–39	3	3	$\frac{1}{10}$
40–49	5	8	$\frac{1}{6}$
50–59	8	16	$\frac{4}{15}$
60–69	10	26	$\frac{1}{3}$
70–79	4	30	$\frac{2}{15}$

1. 30
2. 10
3. 4.6, 4.6, 4.8, 5.1, 5.2, 5.2, 5.2, 5.3, 5.4, 5.4, 5.4, 5.5, 5.6, 5.6, 5.7, 5.8, 5.9, 5.9, 6.0, 6.1

Heights of Students in a Class			
Height, in Feet	Frequency	Cumulative Frequency	Relative Frequency
4.5–4.9	3	3	15%
5.0–5.4	8	11	40%
5.5–5.9	7	18	35%
6.0–6.5	2	20	10%

4. 20
5. 5.0–5.4
6. 10%
7. 90%

Lesson 4.7, page 63

1. 73, 91
2. 115
3. 73
4. 42

Lesson 4.7, page 64

1. Keys will vary. Example: 3 | 1 = 31

Stem	Leaves
2	2 6 7 9 9
3	1 2 5
4	4 6 6
5	3 5

2. Keys will vary. Example: 43 | 5 = 435

Stem	Leaves
43	2 5
44	1 2 3
45	1 1 5 5
46	9 9

3. Keys will vary. Example: 5 | 9 = 59

Stem	Leaves
4	0 6 9
5	2 6 6 9 9 9
6	0 0 0 2 3 3 3 3 4 8
7	0 0 2 4 4 6 6
8	0 1 2 3

4. 63 degrees
5. 43 degrees
6. 63 degrees

Lesson 4.8, page 65

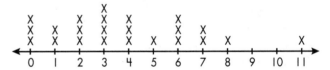

1. 3; 11
2. 23; 3
3. 11

Lesson 4.8, page 66

1. 56 and 57
2. 25
3. 26
4. 56.5
5. Sample answer: from 54 through 60 transactions, because most clerks have been performing within this cluster of transactions
6. Sample answer: above 65 transactions, because a number beyond 65 would be an outlier, indicating an exceptionally high number of transactions

Data Analysis and Probability Answers

Lesson 4.9, page 67
1. 50
2. 10
3. 40
4. 20
5. 25
6. 10; 35
7.
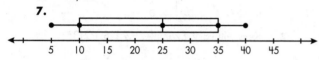

Lesson 4.9, page 68
1. 14
2. 7
3. $15; $24
4. top 50%; the distance from the median to the upper extreme appears greater than to the lower extreme
5. 300
6. 150
7. yes, because 50% of flights carry 300 or more passengers, and planes this size could be responsible for some of the flights carrying fewer than 300

Lesson 4.10, page 69
1. 12
2. pounds
3. 247
4. 280
5. 250
6. 239
7. 280
8. 250
9. mean
10. The mean would increase.
11. The mode would not change.
12. The median would not change.
13. 250
14. 280

Lesson 4.10, page 70
1. Seattle
   a. Seattle's interquartile range and overall range span a narrow set of mild temperatures.
   b. Seattle's temperatures cluster compactly in a mild range.
2. Cleveland
   a. Cleveland has wider ranges and extremes.
   b. Cleveland has temperature clusters at the low end and at the higher end.
3. stem-and-leaf (means cannot be determined from box-and whisker plots)
4. probably box-and-whisker because the median is marked, but some students might prefer using the actual data provided in the stem-and-leaf plot
5. stem-and-leaf (modes cannot be determined from box-and whisker plots)
6. probably box-and-whisker because of its visual representation, but some students might prefer to consider the data clustering provided by the stem-and-leaf in their analysis of spread

Check What You Learned, page 71

1.
	a	b	c
mean:	22.8	28.7	9.1
median:	20	15	8
mode:	18	0	3, 4, 12
range:	41	113	17

2. mean
3. a. $\dfrac{24 + 20 + 26 + 14 + 18 + n}{6} = 20$

   b. 18
4. a. $\dfrac{n}{24} = 65$

   b. 1,560
5. Keys will vary. Example: 22 | 7 = 227

Stem	Leaves
22	2 7
23	5 6 9
24	3 4
25	1 6
26	0 7

6. none
7. 243
8. 222
9. 45

Data Analysis and Probability Answers

Check What You Learned, page 72

10.

Minutes	Frequency	Cumulative Frequency	Relative Frequency
30–34	4	4	26.7%
35–39	2	6	13.3%
40–44	7	13	46.7%
45–49	2	15	13.3%

11.

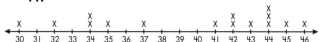

12.

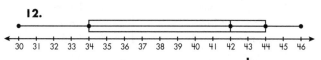

	a	b
13.	39.5	16
14.	42	46
15.	44	30
16.	34	10

Check What You Know, page 73

1.

Annual Product Exports			
Country	Sales (millions)	%	Degrees
Germany	$12	24%	86.4°
Great Britain	16	32%	115.2°
France	10	20%	72.0°
Canada	7	14%	50.4°
China	4	8%	28.8°
Korea	1	2%	7.2°
Total:	**$50**	**100%**	**360°**

Annual Product Exports
Total: $50 Million

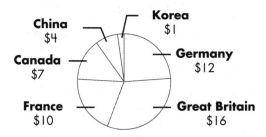

2. investment dollars by age group
3. a 15-year age group
4. 65–80 age group
5. investment dollars, in millions
6. 80–95 age group

Check What You Know, page 74

7.

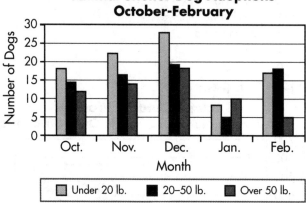

8. the number of new dog arrivals and adoptions from October–February
9. November and January
10. the age of homes and their selling price
11. no
12. no correlation

Lesson 5.1, page 75

1. June; February
2. 1,727; 66.8%
3. 857; 33.2%

Lesson 5.1, page 76

1. units sold over $400, units sold $200–399, and units sold under $200
2. a. units over $400 b. 675
3. 21.1%

Lesson 5.2, page 77

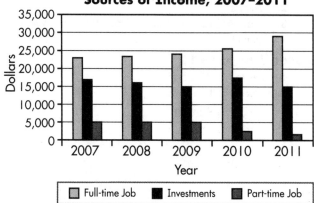

1. $44,767; $44,604
2. His other sources of income decreased.

Data Analysis and Probability Answers

Lesson 5.3, page 78
1. 11.5–12.0
2. 11–11.5
3. number of employees
4. driving miles
5. 72
6. 31

Lesson 5.4, page 79

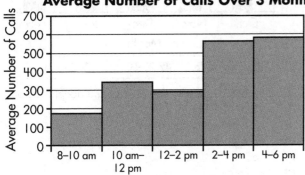

**Leland Outdoor Products
Average Number of Calls Over 3 Months**

1. time periods; average number of calls
2. 100
3. 10 am–12 pm, 2–4 pm, 4–6 pm

Lesson 5.5, page 80
1. academic year enrollment
2. an increase in enrollment
3. Enrollment is flat from 2008–2009 to 2009–2010.
4. 32% increase
5. 3,605

Lesson 5.5, page 81
1. Venice
2. Miami
3. Plant A: Week 4; Plant B: Week 3; Plant C: Week 5
4. Plant C

Lesson 5.6, page 82
1. Sector A: 40% or 144°
2. Sector B: 10% or 36°
3. Sector C: 30% or 108°
4. Sector D: 20% or 72°

5.

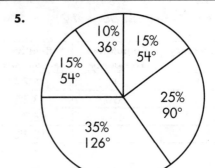

Lesson 5.6, page 83
1.

Income Source	Percent
Property Tax	58.2%
Interest from Reserve Fund	9.2%
Sales Tax	17.4%
Permits and Fees	5.1%
Fines	2.2%
State Grants	4.4%
Federal Grants	3.5%

2. property tax
3. 7.9%
4. more income than expenses: $1,184,515

Check What You Learned, page 84
1.

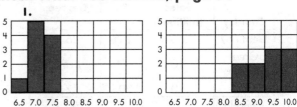

**Mountain Hiking Online Magazine
Subscribers by Age Group, 2007–2010**

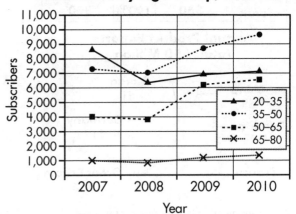

2. 20–35 age group; 65–80 age group
3. 2008
4. 35–50 and 50–65 age groups

Data Analysis and Probability Answers

Check What You Know, page 85

1. Test Scores and Hours of Study
2. positive
3. a student was not studying effectively
4.

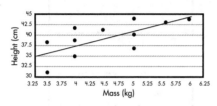

5. Height of dogs and Mass of dogs
6. positive
7. some dogs have a thinner build depending on their breed
8. $20\frac{2}{7}$ centimeters

Lesson 6.1, page 86

1. number of sales agents (x axis) to housing units sold per week (y axis)
2.

Barker Real Estate Sales Agents and Units Sold

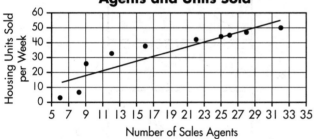

As the number of sales agents increases, the housing units sold per week increase.

Lesson 6.1, page 87

1. outlier
2. negative correlation
3. Sales of those pictures would increase.

Lesson 6.2, page 88

1.

Age and Exercise

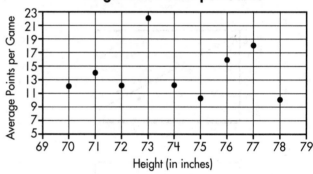

2. The scatter plot shows a negative correlation. As age increases, minutes of daily exercise decrease.
3. 0–20 min. per day
4. There is no correlation.

Carter High School Basketball Team Height and Points per Game

Lesson 6.3, page 89

1. 15 16 17 18 18 20 21 22 23 24
   75 70 75 65 80 75 80 85 80 85
2. negative; no relationship; positive
3.

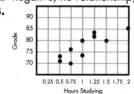

Note: student answers may vary depending on intervals chosen for axis labels.

Data Analysis and Probability Answers

Lesson 6.3, page 90

1. age and height
2. positive
3. 30
4. People stop growing after a certain age.
5. Price of Entrée and Number of Entrees Ordered
6. negative
7. Some expensive entrees are still popular.
8. Possible answer: People will pay a lot for certain house specialties.

Lesson 6.4, page 91

1a.

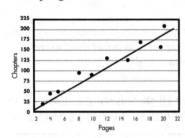

1b.

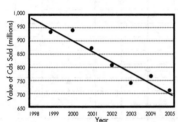

2a.

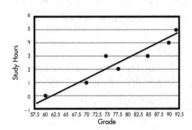

2b.

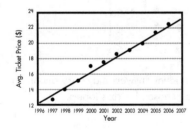

3a.

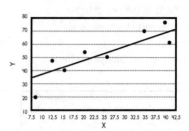

3b.

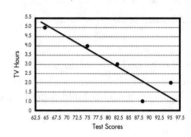

Lesson 6.4, page 92

1a.

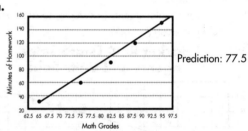

Prediction: 77.5

1b.

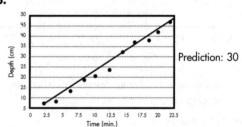

Prediction: 30

2a.

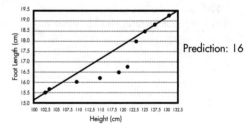

Prediction: 16

2b.

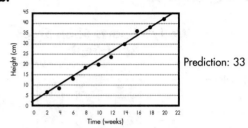

Prediction: 33

3a.

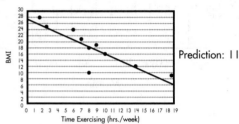

Prediction: 11

3b.

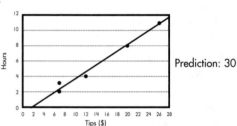

Prediction: 30

Lesson 6.5, page 93
Answers will vary.

       a   **b**

1. $y = 3x - 1$ $y = 75x - 200$

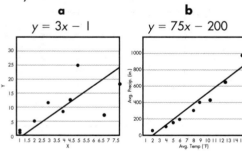

Lesson 6.5, page 94
Answers will vary.

       a   **b**

1. $y = \frac{8}{3}x + 18$ $y = \frac{4}{50}x - 6\frac{1}{5}$

The slope gives the number of points a test score increases per hour.
The y-intercept is the score you would be expected to get if you studied 0 hours.

The slope gives the increase in the number of schools for each increase in population.
The y-intercept is meaningless because it is negative.

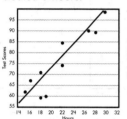 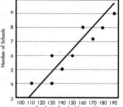

2. $y = 16\frac{2}{3}x + 125$ $y = 2\frac{1}{2}x + 17$

The slope gives the increase in temperature for each increase in sales.
The y-intercept represents the temperature when the amount of sales is zero.

The slope gives the increase of amount of time in the sun for each increase in height.
The y-intercept represents the height of a plant when the amount of time in the sun is 0.

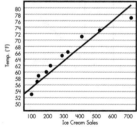 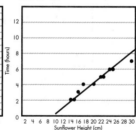

Data Analysis and Probability Answers

Lesson 6.5, page 95
Answers will vary.

a
1. $y = 166\frac{2}{3}x - 133\frac{1}{3}$

The slope gives the amount the cost of a job increases per hour. The y-intercept is meaningless because it is negative.

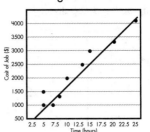

b
$y = -\frac{4}{5}x + 20$

The slope gives the decrease in score per hour. The y-intercept is the score when time equals 0.

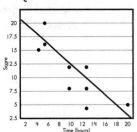

2. $y = 2x + 15$

The slope gives the increase in money per hour. The y-intercept is the amount of money when time equals 0.

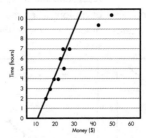

$y = 4.28x + 8$

The slope gives the increase in height for each increase in distance. The y-intercept represents the height when the distance is 0.

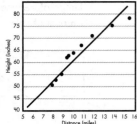

Lesson 6.6, page 96
1.

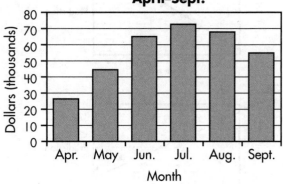

Wally's Sports Shop Sales April–Sept.

2. July
3a. Jackson
3b. Willow
3c. Tramore, Jackson
3d. 18

Lesson 6.6, page 97
4a. $1,800
4b. 38%
5a. January, May, June
5b. February, March
6. between 2.5 and 2.6 lbs.

Fish Weights

Lesson 6.7, page 98
1.

	Europe	Not Europe	Total
South America	120	190	310
Not South America	330	360	690
Total	450	550	1,000

2. 330
3. 360

Data Analysis and Probability Answers

Lesson 6.7, page 99

1.

	Spanish	Not Spanish	Total
French	0.12	0.19	0.31
Not French	0.33	0.36	0.69
Total	0.45	0.55	1.00

2. 0.19
3. 0.12

Check What You Know, page 100
Answers will vary.

1.

a $y = \frac{13}{9}x + 19\frac{5}{9}$

b $y = \frac{5}{2}x + 25$

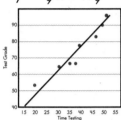
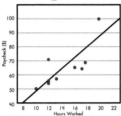

2.

	Run	Do Not Run	Total
Swim	35	65	100
Do Not Swim	125	25	150
Total	160	90	250

3. 65
4. 125
5. 35

Final Test (Chapters 1–6), page 101

1. 6
2. $\frac{1}{6}$
3. $\frac{1}{2}$
4. $\frac{1}{2}$
5. $\frac{1}{6}$
6. $\frac{11}{16}$
7. $\frac{1}{12}$
8. $\frac{20}{77}$

	a	b	c	d
9.	9.2	8	8	5
10.	22.7	22.5	none	18
11.	10.25	12	13	15

Final Test (Chapters 1–6), page 102

12. yes
13. no
14. yes
15. no
16. no
17. $\frac{1}{3}$
18. $\frac{1}{4}$
19. $\frac{1}{2}$
20. $\frac{1}{2}$
21. $\frac{5}{24}$

Final Test (Chapters 1–6), page 103

22. $\frac{9}{400}$
23. $\frac{9}{10}$
24. $\frac{15}{56}$
25.

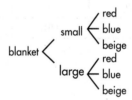

26. $\frac{1}{2}$
27. $\frac{1}{3}$
28. $\frac{1}{6}$
29. 4
30. 8
31. 4.5
32. 24

Final Test (Chapters 1–6), page 104

33. sources of Jan Farmer's 2010 income
34. her full-time job
35. Jan Farmer's income, expenses, and savings, 2007–2011
36. 2008
37. 2011
38. 2008–2011
39. statistical
40. statistical
41. not
42. statistical

Data Analysis and Probability Answers

Final Test (Chapters 1–6), page 105

43. biased
44. biased
45. random
46. year 2
47. (5, 300)
48. positive

Final Test (Chapters 1–6), page 106

49. $\frac{1}{2}$

50.

	Donate	Not Donate	Total
Phone	32	38	70
Email	30	120	150
Total	62	158	220

51.

	Club	No Club	Total
Juniors	150	60	210
Seniors	70	120	190
Total	220	180	400

52. $\frac{7}{19}$